It's Turnaround Time

Cheryl January

ISBN: 979-8-218-90922-2

DEDICATION

This book is dedicated to industry workers worldwide who spend a significant portion of their lives in the workplace. It is my prayer that through the guidance of Jesus Christ, this book will provide hope, strength, and most importantly, salvation.

ACKNOWLEDGMENTS

The Midwives who assisted in giving birth
to this book are gratefully acknowledged. I also
extend sincere appreciation to Cynthia Toliver for her
editing support.

I am thankful for the Women of Valour whose
encouragement inspired me to write within this genre
and helped bring this book to completion.

Contents

Introduction

Welcome to a transformative journey where the worlds of chemical plant work and spiritual growth converge. "It's Turnaround Time" invites you to explore the profound parallels between the meticulous processes of a chemical plant turnaround and the ongoing transformation of our lives under the guidance of God.

Proverbs 16:9 (NIV) sets the foundation for our exploration: "In their hearts humans plan their course, but the Lord establishes their steps." This verse encapsulates the essence of my book, an acknowledgment that, whether in the realm of industry or spirituality, our steps are directed by God.

As we delve into the parallels, consider the structured timeline of a chemical plant turnaround. Just as workers meticulously plan and execute each step to minimize downtime, we too, trust in God's perfect timing. Our faith journey is marked by a divine schedule, and just like a chemical plant turnaround manager orchestrates the steps, we surrender to the Master Planner.

Ecclesiastes 3:1 (NIV) echoes in our hearts: "There is a time for everything, and a season for every activity under the heavens." In this spiritual turnaround, we embrace the seasons of growth, understanding that God's transformative work in our lives is ongoing. We recognize the timeless nature of His renewal and surrender to the divine schedule that shapes our journey.

The parallels extend beyond timing. Romans 12:2 (NIV) calls us to "be transformed by the renewing of your mind." This transformation is not limited to the material world but encompasses our very souls. We recognize the cleansing, reassembly, and optimization themes found both in the physical and the spiritual. The book unfolds as a guide, illustrating how these principles can impact our personal and spiritual growth.

In the spirit of preventive maintenance, we turn to divine promises as our guarantee. Just as a chemical plant relies on preventive measures, our spiritual lives find assurance in promises like Jeremiah 29:11 (NIV): "I know the plans I have for you, 'declares the LORD, 'plans to prosper you and not to harm you, plans to give you hope and a future.'"

Come with me as I dive into the abundance of knowledge in both the manufacturing industry and the Bible to discover declarations, prayers, and insights. The message of "It's Turnaround Time" is an encouragement to align our actions with God's, to wait patiently for God's timing, and to bear witness to a transformation that goes far beyond the physical world.

May this journey inspire you to declare, in the midst of any turnaround, "I trust in God's perfect timing, surrender to His divine schedule, and embrace the ongoing transformation of my life. It's truly turnaround time."

It's Turnaround Time

At work, I was standing on a platform in the center of the chemical plant early one morning after praying and thanking God. The day was uncommonly clear, and the air was heavy with the hardworking energy of the factory workers dismantling a massive distillation column. It was a turnaround, a crucial process in the industrial sector.

Purging the vessel was an essential first stage in the turnaround process since it allowed for a thorough cleaning. The laborers decommissioned the column, every second of their job meticulous and important. After that, they disassembled the column, piece by piece. The air was heavy with perspiration and dust, yet there was also an immediate sense of hope and restoration.

Following the dismantling of the column, each component was pressure-washed to bring it back to its former, shining condition. Then, step by step, the crew started to reassemble the vessel with attention and accuracy. Once every component was replaced in its proper location, this worn distillation column was restored and prepared to fulfill its original function.

I stood there watching this complex process, and then I had a flash of realization. Not only was the column transforming, but life itself was also receiving a deep lesson. That was when I heard God say, "It's

Turnaround Time," in a whisper that was unmistakable in my heart.

It became clear to me in that holy moment that the turnaround I was witnessing was a metaphor for life itself rather than just a column and set of procedures. Sometimes we need to purge and clean our lives as well; we need to break old patterns and habits and disassemble things that no longer serve us. And just as the laborers painstakingly pressure washed and put the column back together, so too may we go through a transformational process to become whole again, rejuvenated, and prepared to serve our purpose.

The realization that life, like production, can be full of processes of restoration and change, is the key concept of "It's Turnaround Time." The transformation we see at work can be a potent reminder that we, too, possess the strength to dismantle, purify, and reconstruct our own lives if we have faith and perseverance. This book will walk you through the processes of personal and spiritual transformation and demonstrate that it's never too late to accept new life, development, and a stronger relationship with God.

A turnaround is about more than just making changes; it's about renewal and a new start. Just as the turnaround rendered the distillation column refreshed and radiant, we too can emerge with a new inner brightness from the purifying of our spirits. Just as the laborers dismantle and clean every part of the column, God's turnaround offers us the chance to let go of the burdens of the past. By doing this, we open the door to a spiritual transformation that goes beyond this world and into the core of our souls and minds.

After making a full recovery, the distillation column can now produce commodities of a high caliber. Similarly, when we allow God to cleanse and rebuild our lives, we become instruments of His grace, able to design a life that reflects His love, truth, and purpose. This metamorphosis is not merely a temporary change. It is a fundamental transformation in our identity that allows us to live as the new creatures God intended us to be. Our lives are enhanced, from our connections with loved ones to our relationship with God.

I invite you to embark on this amazing journey of restoration, growth, and a closer relationship with God. Guided by the vivid metaphor of the unclean vessel and the changes it goes through, we'll learn doable techniques to purify our hearts, thoughts, and spirits, toward a happier, more purposeful future.

Decrees And Declarations

"I decree and declare that, just as the distillation column in manufacturing was cleansed and renewed, I too am cleansed and made new by the grace of God."

Scripture: 2 Corinthians 5:17 (NIV)"Therefore, if anyone is in Christ, the new creation has come: The old has gone, the new is here!"

I decree and declare that God's cleansing power will remove the impurities from my life, just as the workers pressure-washed the vessel in the petrochemical unit, restoring it to its original gleaming state."

Scripture: Psalm 51:7 (NIV)"Purge me with hyssop, and I shall be clean; wash me, and I shall be whiter than snow."

"I decree and declare that my life is a vessel of God's grace, and I am being reassembled with precision, purpose, and dedication by His divine hands."

Scripture: Isaiah 64:8 (NIV)"But now, O Lord, you are our Father; we are the clay, and you are our potter; we are all the work of your hand."

I decree and declare that my spiritual turnaround is not just about changing, but a rebirth and rejuvenation, much like the distillation column in manufacturing."

Scripture: Ezekiel 36:26 (NIV)"I will give you a new heart and put a new spirit in you; I will remove from you your heart of stone and give you a heart of flesh."

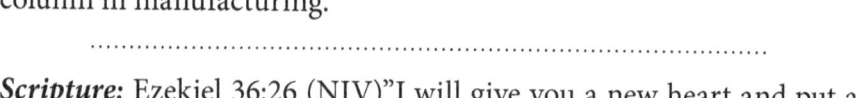

"I decree and declare that I am ready to produce a life that reflects God's love, purpose, and truth, just as the cleansed distillation column is ready to produce high-quality products."

Scripture: Ephesians 2:10 (NIV) "For we are God's handiwork, created in Christ Jesus to do good works, which God prepared in advance for us to do."

Prayer

Father,

As we think about the similarities between the distillation column's turnaround and the spiritual metamorphosis we seek, we are reminded of your wisdom and your unwavering grace, love and dedication to our well-being.

Lord, please grant us commitment and tenacity like the workers who diligently restored the column. May we, too, approach life's restoration with unshakable dedication, understanding that it is an act of love directed by your divine care. As the workers did with the vessel, help us to perfectly reassemble the fragments of our lives, knowing that your hand is guiding each step.

The picture of the vessel coming back to life is a powerful illustration of your ability to turn something old and tarnished into something brand-new and brilliant. Lord, we ask for the grace to accept the limitless opportunity for renewal that you provide, even if we may occasionally feel battered or worn out. When we let you clean and rebuild our lives, may we shine brightly in the roles and purposes you have for us.

Father, we accept the spiritual transformation you have in store for us. With thanks, we accept this invitation, understanding that you will be guiding and reviving us every step of the way.

We ask for clarity and discernment to implement the concepts of a turnaround in our lives; from relationships to personal development to, above all, our individual relationship with you, Lord. We beseech you for direction and for purifying our hearts, minds, and souls with your transformative touch.

Father, give us the strength and courage to let go of the past and welcome the bright future you have planned. We pray that this spiritual transformation will penetrate our being and help us become the new person you have created.

We are grateful for your unwavering love and the assurance of a new life. We offer this prayer in the name of your Son, Jesus Christ.

Amen.

- 2 -

Turnaround Team

In the context of high-performance organizations and manufacturing turnarounds, teambuilding is a cornerstone of success. It's a recognition that no matter how skilled an individual may be, the collective effort of a team is often required to bring a project to successful completion. In the case of a turnaround, it takes a coordinated group of employees with distinct roles and expertise to make it happen. This group often includes the turnaround manager, engineering, maintenance personnel, planners, health and safety coordinators, production managers, supervisors, and other key team members. They are interdependent on one another, and their collaboration and cohesion create a productive and effective team.

In the biblical context, we find the importance of teamwork through Jesus and His disciples. Just as high-performance organizations rely on team dynamics for success, Jesus, during His earthly ministry, selected a team of disciples who would accompany Him and carry His message to the world. The number chosen was twelve, and they formed a close-knit team that supported each other, learned from Jesus, and ultimately played a crucial role in changing the world with the message of love, redemption, and salvation.

Team Dynamics in Industry

In an industrial context, teamwork is a fundamental principle. This aligns with biblical wisdom that encourages the collective effort of believers to achieve great things. In Ecclesiastes 4:9-12 (NIV), it is stated: "Two are better than one because they have a good return for their labor. If either of them falls down, one can help the other up. But pity anyone who falls and has no one to help them up. Also, if two lie down together, they will keep warm. But how can one keep warm alone? Though one may be overpowered, two can defend themselves. A cord of three strands is not quickly broken."

This passage underscores the importance of collaboration and support in achieving common goals. In manufacturing, individuals with different skills and expertise come together to accomplish tasks efficiently and effectively. Just as a team is more than the sum of its parts, a unified group can achieve feats that are challenging for individuals alone.

Jesus and His Disciples

During His ministry, Jesus carefully chose His disciples. These twelve men formed a team that followed Him, learned from Him, and contributed to His mission. Just as teamwork is essential in manufacturing turnarounds, Jesus recognized the power of collaboration in spreading His message of salvation.

In Mark 3:14 (NIV), it is written: "He appointed twelve that they might be with him and that he might send them out to preach." This verse emphasizes two aspects of Jesus' approach to teambuilding: companionship and shared mission. Jesus didn't select His disciples merely for their skills but also for their companionship. They were to be with Him, learning and growing together. Additionally, they were sent out to share the message of the Gospel with the world, highlighting the importance of a collective mission.

Your Family as Your Team

In our daily lives, our family members often form our primary team. They are the ones we rely on for support, companionship, and shared experiences. Just as an industrial team combines their strengths to achieve common goals, our families work together to navigate life's challenges and triumphs.

Proverbs 17:17 (NIV) beautifully captures the essence of familial teamwork: "A friend loves at all times, and a brother is born for a time of adversity." This verse emphasizes the loyalty and support that family members offer in times of difficulty. Your friends, spouse, and children are your team. You need them, and they need you. Together, you combine your strengths to help each other grow, overcome obstacles, and make a positive impact on the world.

Whether in the context of manufacturing turnarounds, Jesus and His disciples, or your family, teamwork is a powerful and essential concept. It is a reminder that we are not meant to navigate life's challenges alone but to join forces with others, leveraging our collective strengths and efforts to achieve common goals and make a meaningful impact on the world. Just as Jesus chose His disciples to carry His message to the world, we are called to collaborate with our family and others, working as a team to grow, thrive, and make a difference.

Decrees and Declarations

"I decree and declare that I will recognize the importance of teamwork in both my professional and personal life, understanding that just as an industrial team collaborates for success, my family and friends are my invaluable team."

"I decree and declare that, like Jesus carefully selected His disciples for companionship and a shared mission, I will invest in building strong, supportive relationships with my loved ones, creating a united team."

....

"I decree and declare that I will embrace the biblical wisdom that 'two are better than one,' as mentioned in Ecclesiastes 4:9 (NIV), and actively seek opportunities for collaboration and support within my team."

....

"I decree and declare that I will draw strength and inspiration from the cord of unity described in Ecclesiastes 4:12 (NIV), recognizing that together, we are stronger and less easily broken by life's challenges."

....

"I decree and declare that, just as Jesus appointed His disciples to be with Him and to share His message, I will be a source of companionship, encouragement, and support to my family, working together to achieve common goals."

....

These decrees and declarations reflect a commitment to recognizing the importance of teamwork in our professional and personal lives, drawing inspiration from both manufacturing team dynamics and the example of Jesus and His disciples. They emphasize the value of collaboration, unity, and shared missions in our relationships with family and friends.

Prayer

Father,

As we reflect on the importance of teamwork and collaboration in our lives, we turn to your Word for guidance and inspiration. In Ecclesiastes 4:9-12 (NIV), we are reminded that two are better than one, for they have a good return for their labor, and a cord of three strands is not quickly broken. We seek your presence and wisdom as we pray for the strength and unity of our teams.

Lord, we recognize the significance of teamwork not only in our workplaces but also within our families, among our friends, and in our communities. Just as manufacturing teams collaborate to achieve common goals, we too strive to work harmoniously with others, leveraging our collective strengths to overcome challenges and achieve great things.

We reflect on the example of Jesus and His disciples, as mentioned in Mark 3:14 (NIV), where Jesus appointed twelve to be with Him and to share His message. We are inspired by the unity and shared mission of this team. We pray for the bonds of companionship and shared purpose to grow stronger within our teams.

Our families are often our primary teams, supporting us in times of adversity and sharing in our joys and triumphs. We take to heart the message of Proverbs 17:17 (NIV), where a friend loves at all times, and a brother is born for a time of adversity. We ask for your blessings upon our families, so that they may continue to be a source of love, support, and strength.

Father, we pray for unity, understanding, and love to flourish within our teams. May we be bound by the cord of unity, as described in Ecclesiastes 4:12 (NIV), ensuring that we stand strong against life's challenges. Just as a manufacturing team combines its strengths to achieve common goals, we also seek to combine our efforts for the betterment of our families, friendships, and communities.

May our teams be sources of inspiration, encouragement, and empowerment, just as your disciples were to Jesus. Help us to recognize the value of teamwork, companionship, and shared missions, and grant us the wisdom to nurture these qualities in our lives.

In your name, we pray.

Amen.

Timing

Timing of the Turnaround

A chemical plant turnaround, as used in manufacturing and industrial operations, is a well-defined procedure that usually takes several weeks to complete. During this period, the plant goes through several important maintenance and restoration tasks. On the other hand, the length of spiritual turnarounds varies significantly and is less predictable. Let's see what the Bible says about time and change to understand the differences and similarities between these two kinds of turnarounds.

The Chemical Plant Turnaround: A Defined Schedule

A chemical plant turnaround is a strategic endeavor. It entails stopping all operations, disassembling, inspecting, cleaning, repairing, replacing, and reassembling parts and equipment, as well as extensively testing the plant's systems. The exact length of a chemical plant turnaround depends on a number of variables, including the facility's size, the nature of the labor involved, and the complexity of the equipment.

The turnaround usually take a few weeks to many months to finish.

The main goals of this procedure are to maximize productivity, improve safety, and guarantee that the facility can continue to produce high-quality goods without disruption. To reduce downtime and guarantee a seamless transition from the shutdown phase to full production, the timing is carefully planned.

The Spiritual Turnaround: A Timeless Journey

A spiritual turnaround is an ongoing, evolving, and very personal journey as opposed to the regimented timeframe of a chemical plant turnaround. A spiritual turnaround can occur over a period of time that is not constrained by weeks or months. Since its central theme is the changing of one's heart, soul, and relationship with God, it transcends earthly limitations and is extremely specific to you.

What Scripture Says About Time in Spiritual Transformation

Scripture frequently makes references to the timeless character of spiritual development. "Therefore, if anyone is in Christ, the new creation has come: The old has gone, the new is here," declares 2 Corinthians 5:17 (NIV). This verse describes the immediate nature of a spiritual turn-around that occurs when a person accepts faith and surrenders to God.

We are reassured in Philippians 1:6 (NIV) that "he who began a good work in you will carry it on to completion until the day of Christ Jesus." Spiritual transformation is a lifelong process of growth and rebirth.

A spiritual turnaround does not have a set duration. It never ends as people walk with God, looking to Him for direction and forgiveness. "Your eyes saw my unformed body; all the days ordained for me were written in your book before one of them came to be," according to Psalm 139:16 (NIV). This passage emphasizes the eternal aspect of spiritual growth and the divine understanding of our life's journey.

The Parallels Between Turnarounds

While the timelines of chemical plant turnarounds and spiritual turnarounds differ significantly, there are remarkable parallels between the two processes. Both involve a deep and transformative cleansing. Cleaning and purging are crucial phases in a chemical plant turnaround. Spiritual turnarounds also entail purging one's heart, mind, and soul so that God can renew and purify them.

Rebuilding and repairing one's faith, connections, and purpose are all part of a spiritual turnaround, much as the reassembly of equipment is in a chemical plant turnaround.

Chemical plants aim to optimize their operations and renew their efficiency. When someone has a spiritual turnaround, they aim to strengthen their faith and restore their relationship with God.

Both kinds of turnarounds are focused on renewal and transformation, although their durations may vary. The New International Version of Romans 12:2 exhorts us to "be transformed by the renewing of your mind." The ideas of material and spiritual turnarounds are echoed in this ongoing process of transformation.

In summary, a spiritual turnaround is a continuous and everlasting journey, whereas a chemical plant turnaround adheres to a set schedule. They both entail renewal, cleansing, and transformation, but they happen over different amounts of time. The similarities between these two kinds of turnarounds show that the concepts of purification, reconstruction, and optimization hold true for both the material world and the spiritual growth and faith realms.

Decrees and Declarations

"I decree and declare that the turnaround of my life is a well-structured process, just as a chemical plant turnaround follows a defined schedule.

Scripture: *Proverbs 16:9 (NIV)* - "In their hearts humans plan their course, but the Lord establishes their steps."

I decree and declare that I embrace the timeless nature of my spiritual turnaround, for God's transformation is ongoing, and I surrender to His divine schedule."

Scripture: *Ecclesiastes 3:1 (NIV)* - "There is a time for everything, and a season for every activity under the heavens."

"I decree and declare just as a chemical plant turnaround is meticulously planned to minimize downtime, I trust that God's timing is perfect, and He will minimize disruptions in my life."

Scripture: *Psalm 37:23 (NIV)* - "The Lord makes firm the steps of the one who delights in him."

"I decree and declare that my spiritual journey is marked by continuous growth, and I surrender to God's guidance throughout my lifetime."

Scripture: *Philippians 1:6 (NIV)* - "he who began a good work in you will carry it on to completion until the day of Christ Jesus."

"I decree and declare that I recognize the parallels between material and spiritual turnarounds, where both involve cleansing, reassembly, and optimization, and I trust in God's transformative power."

Scripture: *Romans 12:2 (NIV)* - "be transformed by the renewing of your mind."

Trust, surrender, and recognition of divine timing are key to spiritual turnarounds. They help us align our journey with God's perfect plan and the ongoing process of transformation in our lives.

Prayer

Heavenly Father,

We acknowledge that you are sovereign over all that concerns us. We understand that our spiritual turnaround occurs according to your divine schedule, just as a chemical plant turnaround occurs according to a set timeline. We know that you set our course and direct us on our journey, so we put our trust in your perfect timing.

Lord, as we look forward to the spiritual turnaround, we seek your wisdom and guidance. May our plans align with your purpose, and may our efforts be efficient and fruitful. We trust that, just as a chemical plant turnaround is meticulously planned to minimize downtime, you will minimize disruptions in our lives, and your hand will be upon every step we take.

Father, we pray according to *Ecclesiastes 3:1 (NIV)* - "There is a time for everything, and a season for every activity under the heavens."

In our spiritual turnaround, we acknowledge the timeless nature of your transformation in our hearts and souls. We surrender to your divine schedule, trusting that you work continuously to renew and refine us. May we embrace the seasons of our spiritual growth, understanding that your timing is perfect and that we are secure in your hands.

Father, we pray according to *Romans 12:2 (NIV)* - "be transformed by the renewing of your mind."

Preventive maintenance is as essential in our spiritual lives as it is in the material world. Lord, we recognize the parallels between material and spiritual turnarounds, where both involve cleansing, reassembly, and optimization. We surrender to your transformative power, inviting You to renew our minds, hearts, and lives. May your Word guide us, and may your Spirit be our constant companion on this journey.

We thank You for the divine promises you've given us, assuring us of your presence and guidance. May we continue to draw strength, wisdom, and renewal from your Word, and may our faith remain unshaken as we navigate both material and spiritual turnarounds. In Jesus' name, we pray. Amen.

- 4 -

The Vessel

In the world of petrochemical units, vessels play a crucial role, much like our lives serve as vessels for our experiences and choices. These vessels, when contaminated or compromised, can lead to problems and off-specification products, much like our lives can be marred by impurities and flaws.

In the petrochemical industry, the importance of keeping vessels clean is paramount, just as the Bible emphasizes the importance of maintaining a clean heart and mind. Proverbs 4:23 (NIV) tells us, "Above all else, guard your heart, for everything you do flows from it." Just as a contaminated vessel can result in off-specification products, a heart and mind tainted with impurities can lead to off-specification thoughts, words, and actions in our lives.

But there is hope, a guiding light of transformation that can purify our lives and restore them to their intended purpose. This light is the divine presence of God, who desires to cleanse and renew us. We are not junk; we are His handiwork, created with intention and love. Ephesians 2:10 (NIV) reminds us, "For we are God's handiwork, created in Christ Jesus to do good works, which God prepared in advance for us to do."

The transformative promise of the Bible in 2 Corinthians 5:17 (NIV) reveals the profound potential for renewal available to us. "Therefore, if anyone is in Christ, the new creation has come: The old has gone, the new is here." This scripture reminds us that when we accept Christ into our lives, a radical transformation occurs. It encompasses our heart, mind, and soul, renewing and purifying every aspect of our being.

The journey of becoming a new creation in Christ is similar to the process of vessel cleaning in the petrochemical unit. Both involve a purposeful, intentional purification. In the petrochemical industry, the cleansing process begins with identifying the impurities. Similarly, in our spiritual lives, we must first acknowledge our need for cleansing and restoration. This recognition is a critical step toward transformation, acknowledging that we are not immune to the impurities that can accumulate within us.

Much like the cleansing process in the petrochemical unit, the purification of our hearts and minds is not always an easy or pleasant experience. It often requires introspection and self-examination, a willingness to face our impurities and imperfections. This can be a challenging but necessary part of the journey toward renewal and becoming the new creations that God envisions us to be.

The process of becoming a new creation also mirrors the meticulous nature of cleaning and refurbishing a vessel. In a petrochemical unit, workers shut down the vessel, disassemble it, and systematically clean every part, piece by piece. This level of precision and attention to detail is essential to restore the vessel to its original condition. In our spiritual journey, we must likewise approach our transformation with diligence, systematically addressing each aspect of our lives.

The pressure washing of the vessel in the petrochemical unit is a powerful symbol of cleansing and renewal. Through God's grace, we, too, can experience a spiritual pressure wash that removes the impurities and stains that have accumulated over time. This process restores us to our original, intended state, making us whiter than snow, as Psalm 51:7 (NIV) expresses, "Cleanse me with hyssop, and I will be clean; wash me, and I will be whiter than snow."

Just as the vessel, once cleansed, is ready to produce high-quality products again, we, when cleansed by God, become vessels of His grace and love, prepared for lives of purpose and impact. The turnaround is not just a concept; it's a tangible reality that offers the promise of spiritual rebirth, transformation, and renewal.

As we continue reading and learning, let us remember that the turnaround is not a one-time event but an ongoing process of becoming the best versions of ourselves. It is a spiritual makeover that transcends the surface and delves deep into our hearts and minds. With each page, we will discover practical steps to cleanse and renew our lives, ultimately leading us toward a brighter, more purposeful future.

Decrees and Declarations

"I decree and declare that I will guard my heart diligently, for it is the wellspring of life, and I will allow God to cleanse it from impurities."

Scripture: Proverbs 4:23 (NIV) - "Above all else, guard your heart, for everything you do flows from it."

"I decree and declare that I am not a vessel of impurity; I am God's handiwork, created for good works and renewed by His grace."

Scripture: Ephesians 2:10 (NIV) - "For we are God's handiwork, created in Christ Jesus to do good works, which God prepared in advance for us to do."

"I decree and declare that, in Christ, I am a new creation; the old has passed away, and I am made new in every aspect of my being."

Scripture: 2 Corinthians 5:17 (NIV) - "Therefore, if anyone is in Christ, the new creation has come: The old has gone, the new is here."

"I decree and declare that, through God's grace, I will undergo a meticulous spiritual cleaning process, dismantling the impurities within me and restoring my heart, mind, and soul to their original condition."

Scripture: Isaiah 1:18 (NIV) - "Come now, let us settle the matter. Though your sins are like scarlet, they shall be as white as snow; though they are red as crimson, they shall be like wool."

"I decree and declare that, just as a vessel, once cleansed, is ready to produce high-quality products, I, too, am prepared to produce the fruits of the Spirit and live a life of purpose."

Scripture: Galatians 5:22-23 (NIV) - "But the fruit of the Spirit is love, joy, peace, forbearance, kindness, goodness, faithfulness, gentleness and self-control. Against such things there is no law."

Prayer

Father,

We come before you with hearts open to your transformative grace. Your Word, Father, reminds us of the profound potential for renewal that is available to us. We pray that you guide us on this journey of cleansing, renewal, and becoming the new creations you desire.

Your Word in Proverbs 4:23 (NIV) instructs us, "Above all else, guard your heart, for everything you do flows from it." We seek your help, Lord, in guarding our hearts, and in acknowledging that impurities can accumulate within us. Help us to recognize the areas in our lives that need cleansing, whether it be thoughts, words, or actions.

Ephesians 2:10 (NIV) reminds us that we are "God's handiwork, created in Christ Jesus to do good works." We declare that we are not vessels of impurity, but vessels of your grace, designed to fulfill the purpose you have prepared for us. May we embrace this truth and live out the good works you have ordained for us.

Your promise in 2 Corinthians 5:17 (NIV) is a beacon of hope: "Therefore, if anyone is in Christ, the new creation has come: The old has gone, the new is here." We decree that we are new creations in Christ, and we cast off the old, embracing the renewal that you offer. May our hearts, minds, and souls be cleansed and transformed by your presence.

Isaiah 1:18 (NIV) declares your willingness to cleanse us: "Come now, let us settle the matter. Though your sins are like scarlet, they shall be as white as snow." We pray for the meticulous cleansing of our hearts, just as a vessel is carefully dismantled and restored. Make us white as snow, Lord, purifying us from all impurities.

Galatians 5:22-23 (NIV) presents the fruits of the Spirit: "But the fruit of the Spirit is love, joy, peace, forbearance, kindness, goodness, faithfulness, gentleness, and self-control." We decree that, through your grace, we will bear these fruits in our lives as vessels of your love and purpose.

Lead us in addressing each aspect of our lives with diligence and purpose, just as workers meticulously cleanse and restore vessels in the petrochemical industry.

May the entire journey be a testament to the reality of spiritual rebirth and transformation. We offer this prayer in the name of your Son, Jesus Christ, who makes all things new.

Amen.

- 5 -

Noise

In the world of manufacturing, particularly in the operation of vessels, noise can be a telltale sign of a problem. Operators are trained to identify and address the root cause of noise, as it often indicates an issue within the vessel's operation. Similarly, in our lives, noise can manifest in the form of negative talk and thoughts, and it too must be addressed and rectified.

The negative chatter and thoughts that permeate our minds can be likened to the noise in a vessel. Just as operators must find and address the root cause of noise in a vessel to prevent shutdowns and disruptions, we must also confront the source of negativity in our lives. This negativity, or "noise," can be detrimental if left unaddressed, as it has the potential to disrupt our emotional and spiritual well-being.

Proverbs 23:7 (KJV) offers a profound insight into the power of our thoughts: "For as he thinketh in his heart, so is he." This verse underscores the significance of our thought life and how it shapes our identity and actions. It serves as a reminder that the thoughts we entertain can influence our character, choices, and ultimately, our destiny.

In the realm of manufacturing, the presence of noise is an indication that something within the vessel's operation is not functioning optimally. Similarly, in our lives, negative noise like self-doubt, criticism from others, or the constant replay of past mistakes, serves as an indicator that something is amiss in our spiritual and emotional well-being. It is a signal that we must pause and seek the root cause of this noise, just as operators do in their work.

Operators address noise by identifying and rectifying the source. We must also take action to combat the negativity that infiltrates our thoughts and spirit. This begins with self-awareness and discernment. We must recognize when the noise is present, acknowledge its impact, and be vigilant in identifying the source of this negative chatter.

Just as workers in a manufacturing environment deal with noise promptly to prevent operational disruptions, we too must address negativity with a sense of urgency. Proverbs 4:23 (NIV) emphasizes the importance of guarding our hearts: "Above all else, guard your heart, for everything you do flows from it." Guarding our hearts and minds from the intrusion of negative noise is paramount for maintaining emotional and spiritual health.

Negativity, much like noise in a vessel, has the potential to cause shutdowns in our lives. It can paralyze us, hinder our personal growth, and impede our relationships. To prevent these shutdowns, we must adopt a proactive approach. We can turn to the wisdom of Philippians 4:8 (NIV), which encourages us to focus on what is true, noble, right, pure, lovely, and admirable: "Finally, brothers and sisters, whatever is true, whatever is noble, whatever is right, whatever is pure, whatever is lovely, whatever is admirable—if anything is excellent or praiseworthy—think about such things."

The practice of renewing our minds with positive and uplifting thoughts is essential in countering the negative noise. Romans 12:2 (NIV) reminds us of the transformative power of renewing our minds: "Do not conform to the pattern of this world, but be transformed by the renewing of your mind. Then you will be able to test and approve what God's will is—his good, pleasing and perfect will."

Workers diligently address noise in vessels to ensure the smooth operation of manufacturing processes. We too must be diligent in addressing the noise in our hearts and minds. The Bible encourages us to "take captive every thought to make it obedient to Christ" (2 Corinthians 10:5, NIV). This active approach involves consciously filtering our thoughts and discarding those that do not align with the truth of God's Word.

By recognizing the presence of noise, identifying its source, and taking active measures to counteract it with positive, uplifting thoughts, we can prevent emotional and spiritual shutdowns

Operators ensure the proper functioning of vessels by addressing noise. We too can ensure our spiritual and emotional well-being by addressing the noise of negativity and replacing it with the truth and wisdom of God's Word. Free from the disruptions caused by negative noise, we can maintain a healthy and harmonious spiritual and emotional life,

Decrees and Declarations

"I decree and declare that I will guard my heart diligently and silence the negative noise that attempts to disrupt my peace and faith."

Scripture: Proverbs 4:23 (NIV) - "Above all else, guard your heart, for everything you do flows from it."

"I decree and declare that my thoughts and focus will align with what is true, noble, right, pure, lovely, and admirable, as encouraged by Philippians 4:8."

Scripture: Philippians 4:8 (NIV) - "Finally, brothers and sisters, whatever is true, whatever is noble, whatever is right, whatever is pure, whatever is lovely, whatever is admirable—if anything is excellent or praiseworthy—think about such things."

"I decree and declare that I will actively renew my mind, rejecting the patterns of negativity and instead embracing the transformative renewal found in Romans 12:2."

Scripture: Romans 12:2 (NIV) - "Do not conform to the pattern of this world, but be transformed by the renewing of your mind. Then you will be able to test and approve what God's will is—his good, pleasing and perfect will."

"I decree and declare that I will take every thought captive and make it obedient to Christ, in line with 2 Corinthians 10:5."

Scripture: 2 Corinthians 10:5 (NIV) - "We demolish arguments and every pretension that sets itself up against the knowledge of God, and we take captive every thought to make it obedient to Christ."

"I decree and declare that I will practice the discipline of addressing and eliminating negative noise in my life, just as diligent workers address noise in vessels to maintain operational efficiency."

Scripture: Proverbs 4:23 (NIV) - "Above all else, guard your heart, for everything you do flows from it."

Prayer

Father,

We come before you in prayer, recognizing the importance of addressing the noise that disrupts our hearts and minds, as discussed in this chapter. Your Word is a lamp to our feet and a light to our path (Psalm 119:105, NIV), and we seek your guidance to navigate the noise and negativity that can hinder our spiritual journey.

Your Word in Proverbs 4:23 (NIV) reminds us to guard our hearts, for everything flows from it. We pray for the wisdom and discernment to recognize the noise in our lives, those negative thoughts and influences that threaten our peace and faith. May we be vigilant in guarding our hearts against this noise.

We declare the truth of Philippians 4:8 (NIV) over our lives, that we will focus on what is true, noble, right, pure, lovely, and admirable. In a world filled with noise, help us fix our thoughts on things that are praiseworthy and in alignment with your Word. Let our minds be a sanctuary of positivity and truth.

Romans 12:2 (NIV) encourages us to be transformed by the renewing of our minds. We pray for this transformative renewal as we combat the noise with the truth of your Word. Help us reject the patterns of negativity and embrace your good, pleasing, and perfect will.

In 2 Corinthians 10:5 (NIV), we are instructed to take every thought captive and make it obedient to Christ. Lord, grant us the strength and discipline to capture and dispel negative thoughts, replacing them with the truth of your Word. May our minds be obedient to Christ in all things.

Just as diligent workers address noise in vessels to maintain operational efficiency, we decree that we will practice the discipline of addressing and eliminating negative noise in our lives. We pray for the courage to confront the sources of negativity and the determination to maintain emotional and spiritual health.

May your Word be a constant guide and source of strength as we navigate the noise of this world. Lead us in the path of righteousness, as Psalm 23:3 (NIV) assures, "He guides me along the right paths for his name's sake."

We offer this prayer in the name of your Son, Jesus Christ,
Amen.

- 6 -

Power

In the petrochemical unit, a tank that begins to lose power is a sign of impending shutdown. The continuous flow of fluid relies on a steady energy source. Similarly, in our lives, we need a constant source of power to endure the challenges that come our way, especially when working demanding shift jobs.

Consider Donnie, a man whose marriage faced imminent collapse due to a lack of power. The pressure of raising a troubled 16-year-old son, Joshua, fell heavily on his wife's shoulders. She tirelessly juggled school, extracurricular activities, and other responsibilities with their son, while Donnie increasingly withdrew from family life, working excessive overtime and neglecting his role as a husband and father.

The parallel between a tank losing power in a petrochemical unit and a family losing power in their relationships is striking. Just as a tank requires an energy source for a continuous flow of fluid, families need a source of power to sustain love, understanding, and unity. In both cases, the absence of power leads to a shutdown.

The Bible makes numerous references to the importance of staying connected to our ultimate source of power: God. Proverbs 3:5-6 (NIV) encourages us to trust in the Lord with all our hearts and to lean not on our understanding but to acknowledge Him in all our ways. It is through this acknowledgment and connection with God that we find the strength to navigate the challenges of life, even in the face of strained relationships and overwhelming responsibilities.

Donnie's story serves as a powerful reminder that we must remain anchored to our spiritual energy source. Neglecting this connection, just like a tank losing power, can have dire consequences in our personal lives. We are reminded in Isaiah 40:31 (NIV) that "those who hope in the Lord will renew their strength." Our hope in God is the source of power that can rejuvenate us when we are drained by life's demands.

The notion of maintaining power is not only applicable to families but also extends to the workplace. Shift workers, in particular, experience the challenges of maintaining a healthy work-life balance. Long hours and irregular schedules can leave them physically and emotionally drained.

Galatians 6:9 (NIV) reminds us to "not become weary in doing good, for at the proper time we will reap a harvest if we do not give up." The power to persevere, even in the face of exhaustion and challenges, comes from our connection to God. We must continuously seek His guidance and strength to maintain our power, both at work and in our personal lives.

As the story of Donnie's family illustrates, a lack of power can lead to breakdowns in communication, understanding, and love. Ephesians 5:25 (NIV) calls husbands to love their wives just as Christ loved the church, demonstrating a sacrificial love that is only possible through a connection with the ultimate source of love and power, God.

The importance of family unity and power is echoed in 1 Corinthians 12:25 (NIV): "so that there should be no division in the body, but that its parts should have equal concern for each other." When family members stay connected to their spiritual energy source, they can support one another, even in the face of challenges.

1 Corinthians 16:14 (NIV) provides a guiding principle: "Do everything in love." The power to work diligently, support our colleagues, and maintain a balanced life comes from a

foundation of love, rooted in our connection with God.

Individuals and families need to stay connected to their ultimate source of power. Just as a tank requires an energy source to prevent shutdown, we need God as our source of strength, love, and perseverance.

When challenges arose, rather than press in, Donnie chose to pull away. Rather than power up, Donnie chose to power down. Donnie serves as a great reminder that even in the face of challenges, it is possible to find renewal and restoration by staying connected to the energy source of our faith. With God's power, we can overcome the obstacles that threaten our relationships, our work-life balance, and our sense of purpose.

We must maintain our spiritual connection and draw on the ultimate source of power, God, so that our families and our work lives can continue to flow with love, resilience, and unity.

Decrees and Declarations

I decree and declare that I will stay connected to my ultimate source of power, God, as He renews my strength and endurance."

Scripture: Isaiah 40:31 (NIV) - "but those who hope in the Lord will renew their strength. They will soar on wings like eagles; they will run and not grow weary, they will walk and not be faint."

"I decree and declare that I will not grow weary in my efforts, both in my family life and at work, for I trust in the Lord's promise to sustain me."

Scripture: Galatians 6:9 (NIV) - "Let us not become weary in doing good, for at the proper time we will reap a harvest if we do not give up."

"I decree and declare that I will love my family sacrificially, just as Christ loved the church, drawing from God's source of love and power."

Scripture: Ephesians 5:25 (NIV) - "Husbands, love your wives, just as Christ loved the church and gave himself up for her."

"I decree and declare that I will support and show equal concern for my family members, preventing divisions and strife within the family unit."

Scripture: 1 Corinthians 12:25 (NIV) - "so that there should be no division in the body, but that its parts should have equal concern for each other."

"I decree and declare that I will approach my work with love and dedication, maintaining a balanced life, drawing strength and power from my faith."

Scripture: 1 Corinthians 16:14 (NIV) - "Do everything in love."

Prayer

Father,

We acknowledge the importance of staying connected to you, our ultimate source of strength and renewal. Your Word reminds us that in our weakness, your power is made perfect (2 Corinthians 12:9, NIV). We come before you in prayer, seeking your divine power to sustain us in our families and workplaces.

Isaiah 40:31 (NIV) reassures us that those who hope in you will renew their strength. We place our hope in you, Lord, trusting that your power will empower us to face the challenges in our lives. May we soar on wings like eagles, run and not grow weary, walk and not be faint.

We declare the promise from Galatians 6:9 (NIV), that we will not grow weary in doing good. We believe in the harvest of blessings that awaits us when we do not give up. Grant us the endurance and strength to persevere in our family life and at work, even in the face of challenges.

We pray for the wisdom and grace to love our families sacrificially, just as Christ loved the church (Ephesians 5:25, NIV). Help us draw from your source of love and power as we strive to strengthen our family bonds and create a loving, unified environment.

Your Word in 1 Corinthians 12:25 (NIV) encourages us to have equal concern for each other, preventing divisions within the family. We pray for unity, understanding, and compassion among our family members. May our relationships be built on the foundation of love and mutual concern.

In our workplaces, we commit to approaching our tasks with love and dedication, as suggested in 1 Corinthians 16:14 (NIV). We ask for your guidance and strength to balance our work and personal lives, drawing on your power to do everything in love.

We understand the importance of staying connected to you, our source of power, so that our families and work lives may continue to flow with love, resilience, and unity. In our moments of weakness, we trust that your power will sustain us, just as 2 Corinthians 12:9 (NIV) assures: "My grace is sufficient for you, for my power is made perfect in weakness."

In the face of challenges and the demands of daily life, help us stay anchored in your love, drawing on your strength and power to guide us. May our families and workplaces be infused with your grace and love, making us instruments of your peace and unity.

We offer this prayer in the name of your Son, Jesus Christ, who is our ultimate source of power and the embodiment of love.

Amen.

Personal Protective Equipment

The importance of personal protective equipment (PPE) is evident in both the workplace and our spiritual journey. In the petrochemical industry, employees are trained to wear gear like earplugs, goggles, hard hats, face shields, nomex, gloves, and steel-toe boots to protect themselves from potential hazards. Failing to wear this equipment puts them at risk of injury. Similarly, in our spiritual walk, we are called to put on the whole armor of God to protect ourselves from the spiritual battles we face daily.

Ephesians 6:13-18 (NIV) provides a profound illustration of this concept, exhorting us to take up the armor of God:

(13) Wherefore take unto the whole armour of God, that ye may be able to withstand in the evil day, and having done all, to stand.

(14) Stand therefore, having your loins girt about with truth, and having on the breastplate of righteousness;

(15) And your feet shod with the preparation of the gospel of peace;

(16) Above all, taking the shield of faith, wherewith ye shall be able to quench all the fiery darts of the wicked.

(17) And take the helmet of salvation, and the sword of the Spirit, which is the word of God:

(18) Praying always with all prayer and supplication in the Spirit, and

watching thereunto with all perseverance and supplication for all saints.

Just as employees don protective gear to safeguard themselves in a hazardous work environment, believers are called to put on the spiritual armor of God to protect themselves from the perils of the spiritual world. Each piece of this divine armor serves a unique purpose.

The Belt of Truth (Ephesians 6:14)

In the workplace, employees wear protective gear like hard hats and goggles to shield themselves from physical harm. In the spiritual realm, the belt of truth is our protection against the deceptions and falsehoods of the enemy. Just as safety gear keeps us secure in the physical world, embracing God's truth safeguards our minds and hearts.

The Breastplate of Righteousness (Ephesians 6:14)

Just as a breastplate guards the vital organs of the body, the breastplate of righteousness shields our spiritual heart from the attacks of the enemy. It reminds us to live a life of righteousness and moral integrity, protecting us from the harmful consequences of sin.

The Shoes of the Gospel of Peace (Ephesians 6:15)

In the workplace, steel-toe boots protect employees' feet from potential hazards. Likewise, the shoes of the gospel of peace prepare us for the spiritual journey. They enable us to walk in peace and share the good news with others, safeguarding us from spiritual dangers.

The Shield of Faith (Ephesians 6:16)

Just as employees use face shields to protect their eyes from debris, the shield of faith guards us against the fiery darts of the enemy. It is our faith that extinguishes the spiritual attacks and doubts that seek to harm us.

The Helmet of Salvation (Ephesians 6:17)

Much like a hard hat protects the head from physical harm, the helmet of salvation safeguards our minds from the enemy's lies and deceptions. It reminds us of our eternal salvation through Christ.

The Sword of the Spirit (Ephesians 6:17)

While in the workplace, employees use tools and equipment to accomplish their tasks, the sword of the Spirit, which is the word of God, is our weapon against spiritual opposition. It is through the Word that we can cut through the enemy's deceptions and darkness.

Persevering in Prayer (Ephesians 6:18)

In the petrochemical industry, employees are trained to be vigilant and watchful. In our spiritual journey, we are called to remain watchful in prayer, supporting and interceding for fellow believers.

Just as employees are at risk when they neglect to wear their personal protective equipment, we are vulnerable in our spiritual walk when we fail to put on the whole armor of God. The spiritual battles we face are just as real as physical hazards, and our spiritual armor is essential for our protection. For safety, employees depend on their gear. Similarly we must depend on God's divine armor to guard us in all aspects of life—on the job, at home, in the community, and even at church.

Decrees and Declarations

"I decree and declare that I will put on the whole armor of God daily, for I understand the spiritual battles I face."

....

Scripture: Ephesians 6:13 (NIV) - "Therefore put on the full armor of God, so that when the day of evil comes, you may be able to stand your ground."

"I decree and declare that I will stand firm with the belt of truth fastened around my waist, guarding my mind and heart from deception."

....

Scripture: Ephesians 6:14 (NIV) - "Stand firm then, with the belt of truth buckled around your waist."

"I decree and declare that I will wear the breastplate of righteousness, protecting my spiritual heart from the attacks of the enemy."

....

Scripture: Ephesians 6:14 (NIV) - "with the breastplate of righteousness in place."

"I decree and declare that I will walk in the shoes of the gospel of peace, spreading the message of Christ's peace and protection."

....

Scripture: Ephesians 6:15 (NIV) - "and with your feet fitted with the readiness that comes from the gospel of peace."

"I decree and declare that I will raise the shield of faith, extinguishing all the fiery darts of the wicked, trusting in God's protection."

....

Scripture: Ephesians 6:16 (NIV) - "In addition to all this, take up the shield of faith, with which you can extinguish all the flaming arrows of the evil one."

⌒

Prayer

Father, we are reminded of the vital importance of putting on the whole armor of God for our spiritual protection. Your Word in Ephesians 6:13-18 (NIV) guides us in this endeavor, and we come before you in prayer, seeking your divine protection.

(13) Wherefore take unto the whole armour of God, that ye may be able to withstand in the evil day, and having done all, to stand.

(14) Stand therefore, having your loins girt about with truth, and having on the breastplate of righteousness;

(15) And your feet shod with the preparation of the gospel of peace;

(16) Above all, taking the shield of faith, wherewith ye shall be able to quench all the fiery darts of the wicked.

(17) And take the helmet of salvation, and the sword of the Spirit, which is the word of God:

(18) Praying always with all prayer and supplication in the Spirit, and watching thereunto with all perseverance and supplication for all saints.

Just as employees in the petrochemical industry rely on personal protective equipment to shield themselves from physical dangers, we depend on the armor of God to safeguard us in the spiritual battles we face.

We declare our commitment to put on the whole armor of God, recognizing the significance of each piece of this divine protection. We gird our loins with the belt of truth, guarding our minds and hearts against the deceptions and falsehoods of the enemy.

We embrace the breastplate of righteousness, shielding our spiritual hearts from the attacks of the devil. May we live lives of moral integrity and righteousness, standing firm against sin.

As we put on the shoes of the gospel of peace, we prepare ourselves to walk in peace and share the good news with others. Help us to be instruments of your peace and protection, even during spiritual battles.

We raise the shield of faith, quenching all the fiery darts of the wicked that seek to harm us. Our faith in you is our ultimate protection and defense.

The helmet of salvation rests upon our heads, guarding our minds against the lies and deceptions of the enemy. We rejoice in the assurance of our eternal salvation through Christ.

We take up the sword of the Spirit, which is the word of God, as our weapon against spiritual opposition. Your Word is our source of truth and discernment.

Lord, we understand that spiritual protection requires constant vigilance, so we commit to praying always with all prayer and supplication in the Spirit. We watch with perseverance and supplication for all our fellow believers.

Just as employees are at risk when they neglect their personal protective equipment, we are vulnerable in our spiritual journey when we fail to put on the whole armor of God. We acknowledge that spiritual battles are real, and your divine armor is essential for our protection.

During our spiritual turnaround, we depend on the whole armor of God. We seek your divine protection in all aspects of life, from our workplaces and homes to our communities and churches. As we navigate these spiritual battles, we rely on your strength and protection.

May your Word, your truth, and your presence be our constant source of protection and guidance. We offer this prayer in the name of your Son, Jesus Christ, who is our ultimate source of strength and protection.

Amen.

- 8 -

Tools

In the journey of spiritual turnaround, just as in a turnaround project within the petrochemical industry, the identification and use of appropriate tools are critical. These tools serve as resources and guidelines to help employees and their families navigate challenges such as divorce, illness, drug abuse, alcoholism, and difficulties with their children. The Spiritual Turnaround Project Team recognized these needs and identified seven essential tools for the turnaround process:

Prayer and Fasting

The power of prayer and fasting is a recurring theme in the Bible. Matthew 17:20 (NIV) tells us that with faith the size of a mustard seed, we can move mountains. Prayer and fasting intensify our connection with God, deepening our faith and allowing us to overcome the most challenging circumstances. Fasting is a spiritual discipline that enhances our sensitivity to the divine, helping us seek God's guidance and strength.

Meditating on the Word

In Psalm 1:2 (NIV), we are encouraged to meditate on God's Word day and night, likening us to trees planted by streams of water. Just as employees in the petrochemical industry rely on the precise use of their tools, meditating on the Word is our tool for nourishing our souls and maintaining a strong, stable foundation. 2 Timothy 3:16-17 (NIV) states, all scripture is God-breathed and is useful teaching, rebuking, correcting and training in righteousness, so that the servant of God may be thoroughly equipped for every good work.

Praise and Worship

In our spiritual journey, the importance of praise and worship cannot be overestimated. Psalm 100:4 (NIV) invites us to enter His gates with thanksgiving and His courts with praise. Praise and worship are tools that help us access God's presence, creating an atmosphere of gratitude, joy, and spiritual growth.

Tithing

Tithing is a practice deeply rooted in biblical tradition, as seen in Malachi 3:10 (NIV), where God calls us to bring our tithes into the storehouse. Tithing serves as a tool to honor God with our finances, trust Him to provide for our needs, and contribute to the well-being of others. Tithing is a tool for managing our resources according to God's principles.

Keep the Faith

The concept of faith is central to our spiritual journey. Hebrews 11:1 (NIV) defines faith as the assurance of things hoped for, the conviction of things not seen. Faith is a tool that enables us to trust God's promises, even when circumstances appear bleak. It empowers us to persevere through life's challenges.

Obedience

Obedience to God's commands is a foundational tool in our spiritual journey. It ensures that we walk in His ways. Deuteronomy 28:1 (NIV) reminds us that if we fully obey the Lord and carefully follow all His commands, blessings will overtake us. Obedience is our tool for aligning with God's will and experiencing the blessings He promises.

Be Filled with the Holy Spirit

Ephesians 5:18 (NIV) instructs us not to be drunk with wine but to be filled with the Spirit. Being filled with the Holy Spirit is a transformative tool that empowers us to live a life characterized by love, joy, peace, patience, kindness, goodness, faithfulness, gentleness, and self-control (Galatians 5:22-23, NIV). It is the tool that enables us to be guided by the Spirit's wisdom and strength.

Just as skilled professionals in the petrochemical industry rely on their tools for precision and effectiveness, these seven spiritual tools—prayer and fasting, meditating on the Word, praise and worship, tithing, keeping the faith, obedience, and being filled with the Holy Spirit are essential for the spiritual turnaround. They empower us to navigate life's challenges, just as industry workers rely on their tools to address technical difficulties.

These tools are not mere suggestions but are essential for the turnaround process. By utilizing them, employees and their families can overcome the challenges they face and experience a profound transformation. These tools are the instruments that guide us in our spiritual journey, just as skilled professionals use their tools for successful project completion.

In the petrochemical industry, the right tools are indispensable for success. In our spiritual journey, the right tools are crucial for experiencing a divine turnaround. These tools empower us to overcome adversity, grow in faith, and find hope and purpose in our lives. As skilled workers trust in the effectiveness of their tools, we too must place our trust in the power of these spiritual tools to guide us through our turnaround process.

Decrees and Declarations

"I decree and declare that I will utilize the powerful tool of prayer and fasting to deepen my connection with God and overcome life's challenges."

Scripture: Matthew 17:20 (NIV) - "Truly I tell you, if you have faith as small as a mustard seed, you can say to this mountain, 'Move from here to there,' and it will move. Nothing will be impossible for you."

"I decree and declare that I will meditate on God's Word day and night, just as Psalm 1:2 (NIV) instructs, to establish a strong and stable foundation for my life."

Scripture: Psalm 1:2 (NIV) - "But whose delight is in the law of the Lord, and who meditates on his law day and night."

"I decree and declare that I will use the tool of praise and worship to access God's presence, fostering an atmosphere of gratitude, joy, and spiritual growth."

Scripture: Psalm 100:4 (NIV) - "Enter his gates with thanksgiving and his courts with praise; give thanks to him and praise his name."

"I decree and declare that I will honor God with my finances through tithing, trusting in His provision and contributing to the well-being of others."

Scripture: Malachi 3:10 (NIV) - "Bring the whole tithe into the storehouse, that there may be food in my house. Test me in this," says the Lord Almighty, "and see if I will not throw open the floodgates of heaven and pour out so much blessing that there will not be room enough to store it."

"I decree and declare that I will keep the faith, trusting in God's promises and persevering through life's challenges."

Scripture: Hebrews 11:1 (NIV) - "Now faith is confidence in what we hope for and assurance about what we do not see."

These decrees and declarations are rooted in the power of God's Word and serve as reminders of the essential tools we need for our spiritual journey and turnaround.

Prayer

Father, we are reminded of the essential spiritual resources and guidelines needed for our journey of turnaround. Your Word provides us with these powerful tools, and we come before you in prayer, seeking your guidance and strength in utilizing them.

Prayer and Fasting

Scripture: Matthew 17:20 (NIV) - "Truly I tell you, if you have faith as small as a mustard seed, you can say to this mountain, 'Move from here to there,' and it will move. Nothing will be impossible for you."

Meditating on the Word

Scripture: Psalm 1:2 (NIV) - "But whose delight is in the law of the Lord, and who meditates on his law day and night."

Praise and Worship

Scripture: Psalm 100:4 (NIV) - "Enter his gates with thanksgiving and his courts with praise; give thanks to him and praise his name."

Tithing

Scripture: Malachi 3:10 (NIV) - "Bring the whole tithe into the storehouse, that there may be food in my house. Test me in this," says the Lord Almighty, "and see if I will not throw open the floodgates of heaven and pour out so much blessing that there will not be room enough to store it."

Keeping the Faith:

Scripture: Hebrews 11:1 (NIV) - "Now faith is confidence in what we hope for and assurance about what we do not see."

Obedience

Scripture: Deuteronomy 28:1 (NIV) - "If you fully obey the Lord your God and carefully follow all his commands I give you today, the Lord your God will set you high above all the nations on earth."

Being Filled with the Holy Spirit

Scripture: Ephesians 5:18 (NIV) - "Do not get drunk on wine, which leads to debauchery. Instead, be filled with the Spirit."

———

We acknowledge the importance of these tools for our spiritual journey. Just as skilled workers in the petrochemical industry rely on their tools for precision and effectiveness, we rely on these spiritual tools to navigate life's challenges and experience a profound transformation.

Lord, we pray for wisdom and discernment to use these tools effectively. May prayer and fasting deepen our connection with you, and meditation on your Word provide us with a strong foundation. Let praise and worship create an atmosphere of gratitude, and tithing help us trust in your provision.

Give us the strength to keep the faith, even when circumstances seem challenging, and help us embrace obedience to your commands. Fill us with your Holy Spirit, guiding us in love, joy, and self-control.

We entrust our spiritual journey to you, dear Lord, knowing that these tools are the instruments that will guide us in our turnaround process. Just as skilled professionals trust in the effectiveness of their tools, we place our trust in the power of these spiritual tools to lead us closer to you.

In Jesus' name, we pray. Amen.

- 9 -

Pressure Washer

In the petrochemical industry, a high-powered pressure washer is a crucial tool used to clean vessels and their components during a turn-around. This powerful tool ensures that all contaminants, residues, and impurities are removed, leaving the vessel in a pristine state. Just as the pressure washer is essential for maintaining the efficiency and integrity of industrial equipment, God's cleansing and purifying work in our lives is a fundamental component of our spiritual journey.

Cleansing and Renewal Through God's Grace

When we turn to God and seek His forgiveness for our sins and iniquities, He performs a divine work within us. Just as a pressure washer removes layers of grime, God's grace cleanses and purifies us. The Bible tells us in Psalm 51:7 (NIV), "Cleanse me with hyssop, and I will be clean; wash me, and I will be whiter than snow." God's forgiveness and grace have the power to wash away the stains and impurities that accumulate in our lives.

Washed in the Blood of the Lamb

In Revelation 7:14 (NIV), we read, "They have washed their robes and made them white in the blood of the Lamb." This powerful imagery illustrates the redemptive and purifying nature of Christ's sacrifice. Just as the pressure washer removes contaminants, the blood of Jesus Christ cleanses us from our sins. When we acknowledge our need for a Savior and accept Jesus into our lives, we experience a transformative cleansing, becoming new creations in Christ.

Pleading the Blood of Jesus Against the Enemy

In the spiritual battles we face, there is a tool that can be likened to a "pressure washer" - the act of pleading the blood of Jesus against the enemy. The Bible reminds us in Revelation 12:11 (NIV), "They triumphed over [the enemy] by the blood of the Lamb." Just as a high-pressure washer forcefully removes stubborn residues, pleading the blood of Jesus is a powerful and forceful declaration of victory over the schemes of the enemy.

When challenges, temptations, and spiritual opposition arise, we have the authority to plead the blood of Jesus as a shield against the attacks of the adversary. This act signifies our trust in Christ's redemptive work and His power to overcome all forms of darkness. It is a spiritual tool that empowers us to stand firm in our faith.

The Pressure Washer of Spiritual Renewal

God's cleansing and purifying work renews and revitalizes our lives. We are not meant to carry the burdens of our sins and shortcomings. Instead, we are invited to surrender them to God, allowing His grace to wash us clean.

This process of renewal and purification is essential for our spiritual well-being. In Romans 12:2 (NIV), we are urged, "Do not conform to the pattern of this world, but be transformed by the renewing of your mind." God's cleansing work in our lives transforms us, enabling us to live in alignment with His will and purpose.

The Power of Surrender

The pressure washer is a powerful tool, but it requires surrender and submission to its force. Similarly, surrendering to God and acknowledging our need for His cleansing and renewal is a fundamental step in our spiritual journey. In 1 John 1:9 (NIV), we find this promise: "If we confess our sins, he is faithful and just and will forgive us our sins and purify us from all unrighteousness."

God's cleansing and purifying work is not contingent on our perfection; it is rooted in His faithfulness and love. Just as industrial equipment is restored to peak performance through the pressure washer's force, our lives are renewed and purified through the unchanging love and faithfulness of our Heavenly Father.

Using the "Pressure Washer" in Spiritual Warfare

When the enemy attempts to attack us with doubts, fears, or temptations, we have the authority to invoke the power of the blood of Jesus. Just as a pressure washer is directed toward contaminants to remove them, we can forcefully declare our victory through the blood of the Lamb. This act of spiritual warfare is a reminder of Christ's redemptive work and our identity as conquerors through Him.

Ephesians 6:12 (NIV) emphasizes the spiritual battles we face: "For our struggle is not against flesh and blood, but against the rulers, against the authorities, against the powers of this dark world and against the spiritual forces of evil in the heavenly realms." Just as skilled workers use the pressure washer to combat stubborn residues, we have a spiritual tool to combat the schemes of the adversary.

God's redemptive work restores our lives, making us whiter than snow. May we embrace the cleansing and renewing work of God's grace and confidently use the spiritual tool of pleading the blood of Jesus in the face of spiritual opposition. May we rely on the cleansing power of God to make us whole, renewed, and transformed.

Decrees and Declarations

"I decree and declare that God's grace cleanses me and makes me whiter than snow, just as Psalm 51:7 (NIV) promises."

Scripture: Psalm 51:7 (NIV) - "Cleanse me with hyssop, and I will be clean; wash me, and I will be whiter than snow."

"I decree and declare that I am washed in the blood of the Lamb, as Revelation 7:14 (NIV) assures, and I am a new creation in Christ."

Scripture: Revelation 7:14 (NIV) - "They have washed their robes and made them white in the blood of the Lamb."

"I decree and declare that, like in Revelation 12:11 (NIV), I triumph over the enemy by the blood of the Lamb, declaring my victory over all darkness."

Scripture: Revelation 12:11 (NIV) - "They triumphed over [the enemy] by the blood of the Lamb."

"I decree and declare that God's cleansing and purifying work transforms me, renewing my mind and aligning me with His will, just as Romans 12:2 (NIV) instructs."

Scripture: Romans 12:2 (NIV) - "Do not conform to the pattern of this world, but be transformed by the renewing of your mind."

"I decree and declare that, in spiritual warfare, I have the authority to invoke the power of the blood of Jesus, as it is written in Ephesians 6:12 (NIV), and I am a conqueror through Him."

Scripture: Ephesians 6:12 (NIV) - "For our struggle is not against flesh and blood, but against the rulers, against the authorities, against the powers of this dark world and against the spiritual forces of evil in the heavenly realms."

These decrees and declarations are rooted in the promises and principles of Scripture, empowering us to embrace God's cleansing, renewal, and victory in our lives.

Prayer

Father,

We are reminded of your incredible cleansing and purifying work in our lives. Your Word assures us that your grace is like a powerful pressure washer, capable of washing away our sins and making us whiter than snow.

Psalm 51:7 (NIV) says, "Cleanse me with hyssop, and I will be clean; wash me, and I will be whiter than snow." We come before you, Lord, acknowledging our need for this cleansing. We desire to be purified and made new by your grace.

Revelation 7:14 (NIV) speaks of being washed in the blood of the Lamb, and we are grateful for the redemptive work of Jesus Christ. We declare that we are new creations in Him, cleansed by His precious blood. Thank you for the transformation and renewal that you bring into our lives.

Revelation 12:11 (NIV) reminds us of our victory through the blood of the Lamb. In the face of spiritual battles and opposition, we have the authority to plead the blood of Jesus, declaring our triumph over the enemy's schemes. Grant us the strength and boldness to do so.

Romans 12:2 (NIV) encourages us to be transformed by the renewing of our minds, and we seek this transformation through your cleansing work. May your grace align us with your will and empower us to live according to your purpose.

Ephesians 6:12 (NIV) reminds us of the spiritual battles we face. We acknowledge our need for the protection and victory that come through the blood of Jesus. In times of spiritual warfare, may we confidently invoke the power of His blood as a shield against darkness.

Heavenly Father, we surrender to your cleansing and renewing work. We submit ourselves to your grace, knowing that it washes us clean and makes us whole. As we confront spiritual opposition, may we boldly plead the blood of Jesus, declaring our victory in Him.

Thank you for being our ultimate Pressure Washer, capable of removing the impurities in our lives. We embrace your cleansing and purifying work with gratitude and humility. May your grace transform us and empower us to stand strong against the enemy.

In Jesus' name, we pray.

Amen.

- 10 -

Equipment

In the petrochemical industry, a successful turnaround heavily relies on a wide range of equipment such as scaffolds, ladders, tie-offs, pumps, hoists, and booms, among others. These tools and apparatuses are essential for disassembling, cleaning, and reassembling the equipment. Without these instruments, a turnaround simply cannot occur.

Likewise, in our spiritual journey of turnaround, God provides us with equipment that is vital for our transformation and growth. This equipment is none other than the fruit of the Spirit. In Galatians 5:22-23 (NIV), it is written, "But the fruit of the Spirit is love, joy, peace, forbearance, kindness, goodness, faithfulness, gentleness and self-control. Against such things there is no law." These attributes, known as the fruit of the Spirit, are indispensable for our spiritual turnaround and personal development.

The Role of Equipment in Turnarounds

In the petrochemical industry, skilled professionals rely on a wide array of equipment to ensure the turnaround process is completed effectively and safely. Scaffolds provide access to hard-to-reach areas, ladders facilitate movement, tie offs secure workers, pumps handle liquids, hoists lift heavy loads, and booms support equipment positioning. Each tool plays a specific role in the restoration and renewal of industrial equipment.

Similarly, God equips us with the fruit of the Spirit to support our spiritual turnaround. Let's explore the significance of each aspect of the fruit of the Spirit:

Love: Love is the foundation of our spiritual journey. As 1 Corinthians 13:13 (NIV) tells us, "And now these three remain: faith, hope and love. But the greatest of these is love." Love binds us to God and one another.

Joy: Joy provides the strength to endure difficulties and trials. Nehemiah 8:10 (NIV) reminds us, "The joy of the Lord is your strength."

Peace: The peace of God transcends understanding and guards our hearts and minds (Philippians 4:7, NIV), providing serenity amidst life's storms.

Forbearance: Also known as patience or longsuffering, it enables us to persevere and tolerate challenges. Colossians 3:12 (NIV) encourages us to "clothe yourselves with compassion, kindness, humility, gentleness, and patience."

Kindness: Kindness, described in Ephesians 4:32 (NIV), encourages us to "be kind and compassionate to one another, forgiving each other, just as in Christ God forgave you."

Goodness: Goodness is a testament to the purity of heart. Matthew 5:8 (NIV) says, "Blessed are the pure in heart, for they will see God."

Faithfulness: Faithfulness, as emphasized in 1 Corinthians 4:2 (NIV), calls for stewards to be "found faithful." It signifies our commitment to God and His purposes.

Gentleness: Gentleness is a characteristic of Christ Himself. As Matthew 11:29 (NIV) states, "Take my yoke upon you and learn from me, for I am gentle and humble in heart, and you will find rest for your souls."

Self-Control: Self-control is the ability to restrain our impulses and make wise choices. Proverbs 25:28 (NIV) reveals, "Like a city whose walls are broken through is a person who lacks self-control."

The Fruit of the Spirit is Essential

Just as each piece of equipment in the petrochemical turnaround process is indispensable, the fruit of the Spirit is essential for our spiritual turnaround. We cannot experience true transformation and growth without the presence and operation of these qualities in our lives.

As skilled workers rely on scaffolds to access elevated areas, we must rely on love to reach new heights of understanding, compassion, and connection with God and others. In the same way that ladders enable movement and access to different parts of the equipment, joy empowers us to navigate the complexities of life with a heart full of delight, regardless of our circumstances. Tie-offs protect workers from falling, and peace safeguards our hearts and minds, keeping us secure in the knowledge of God's sovereignty and care. Pumps handle fluids with precision, and forbearance allows us to handle the fluidity of time, understanding that God's timing is perfect. Hoists lift heavy loads, and kindness lifts the burdens of others, demonstrating the love of Christ. Booms provide support and positioning, just as goodness positions us to reflect God's character in our actions. Faithfulness upholds trust and consistency in our relationship with God and others. Gentleness ensures our interactions are marked by humility and compassion, much like Christ Himself. Self-control empowers us to make wise choices, and exercise discipline and discernment in our daily lives.

May we recognize the significance of each aspect of the fruit of the Spirit and allow them to operate in our lives, shaping us into the image of Christ. Just as workers cannot succeed in a turnaround without their equipment, we cannot experience a true turnaround without the fruit of the Spirit.

Decrees and Declarations

"I decree and declare that I am equipped with the fruit of the Spirit, as

Galatians 5:22-23 (NIV) affirms, and I will bear these fruits in my life."

Scripture: Galatians 5:22-23 (NIV) - "But the fruit of the Spirit is love, joy, peace, forbearance, kindness, goodness, faithfulness, gentleness and self-control. Against such things there is no law."

"I decree and declare that just as equipment is essential for a successful turnaround, the fruit of the Spirit is indispensable for my spiritual transformation and growth."

Scripture: Proverbs 3:3-4 (NIV) - "Let love and faithfulness never leave you; bind them around your neck, write them on the tablet of your heart. Then you will win favor and a good name in the sight of God and man."

"I decree and declare that I will bear good fruit in abundance, reflecting the character of Christ, as mentioned in John 15:5 (NIV)."

Scripture: John 15:5 (NIV) - "I am the vine; you are the branches. If you remain in me and I in you, you will bear much fruit; apart from me you can do nothing."

"I decree and declare that the fruit of the Spirit equips me to navigate life's challenges with grace, joy, and love, regardless of my circumstances."

Scripture: Philippians 4:13 (NIV) - "I can do all this through him who gives me strength."

"I decree and declare that the presence of the fruit of the Spirit in my life positions me to reflect God's character, showing His goodness, kindness, and faithfulness to others."

Scripture: 1 Peter 2:12 (NIV) - "Live such good lives among the pa-gans that, though they accuse you of doing wrong, they may see your good deeds and glorify God on the day he visits us."

These decrees and declarations are rooted in the promises of Scrip-ture, empowering us to embrace the essential equipment for our spiri-tual journey and transformation - the fruit of the Spirit.

Prayer

Father,

Galatians 5:22-23 (NIV) assures us of the fruit of the Spirit, and we desire to bear this fruit abundantly. May these qualities become evident in our lives, reflecting your character and love.

We recognize the indispensability of the fruit of the Spirit in our spiritual journey. We believe, with your guidance, we are well-equipped to navigate the challenges of life.

Proverbs 3:3-4 (NIV) encourages us to let love and faithfulness never leave us. We bind these qualities around our hearts and seek to win favor in your sight and in the eyes of others.

We desire to reflect your character in all we do. John 15:5 (NIV) as-sures that we can do so when we remain in You. May we bear good fruit.

In times of trials and tribulations, we declare that the fruit of the Spirit equips us to find strength and joy, as proclaimed in Philippians 4:13 (NIV). We trust in You to provide the necessary equipment for our spiritual journey.

May the presence of the fruit of the Spirit in our lives position us to reflect your goodness, kindness, and faithfulness to those around us, as mentioned in 1 Peter 2:12 (NIV). We strive to be beacons of your light, glorifying You in all that we do.

Father, we surrender to the work of your Spirit within us, equip-ping us with the attributes needed for our spiritual transformation and growth. We desire to bear this fruit abundantly and to reflect your character in every aspect of our lives.

In Jesus' name, we pray.

Amen.

- 11 -

Extreme Makeover

In the world of manufacturing and petrochemical turnarounds, the process is meticulous and thorough. It involves purging the vessel, disassembling its components, pressure washing, repairing, and finally, reassembling it. The end goal is not just to restore the vessel to its former state but to make it even better, ensuring that it operates within specifications and profitability for the corporation.

Likewise, when God undertakes a turnaround in your life, it's not a mere superficial change. It's an extreme makeover that goes beyond outward appearances. It's not a moment where you need to ask, "How do you like me now?" The transformation God brings is profound and evident to all who encounter you. It involves a complete overhaul of your being, from the inside out.

Ezekiel 36:26 (NIV) tells us, "I will give you a new heart and put a new spirit in you; I will remove from you your heart of stone and give you a heart of flesh." This is the essence of a spiritual makeover – a new heart, a new spirit, and a complete transformation of your innermost self.

The process of a spiritual turnaround is not unlike the steps of an industrial turnaround. Let's explore how God's work mirrors each phase:

Purging: In the purging phase of your life, God cleanses you from the impurities and sins that have built up over time. Psalm 51:7 (NIV) states, "Cleanse me with hyssop, and I will be clean; wash me, and I will be whiter than snow." God removes the old and prepares you for the new.

Disassembling: God dismantles the old, unhealthy patterns, and mindsets that have held you captive. Romans 12:2 (NIV) guides us, "Do not conform to the pattern of this world but be transformed by the renewing of your mind." He disassembles the old to make room for the new.

Pressure Washing: Just as the vessel undergoes a thorough cleansing, God washes you in His Word and grace. Ephesians 5:26 (NIV) says, "to make her holy, cleansing her by the washing with water through the word." His Word purifies and renews you.

Repairing: God heals the brokenness within you. Psalm 147:3 (NIV) reassures us, "He heals the brokenhearted and binds up their wounds." He restores what was damaged.

Reassembling: God puts you back together, but you are not the same as before. 2 Corinthians 5:17 (NIV) declares, "Therefore, if anyone is in Christ, the new creation has come: The old has gone, the new is here!" God rebuilds you as a new creation.

Powering Up: Just as the vessel is powered up and put back online, God empowers you with His Spirit. Acts 1:8 (NIV) promises, "But you will receive power when the Holy Spirit comes on you." You are filled with the power to live out your new life.

The result of a spiritual turnaround is not merely a change in appearance, but a complete transformation of your identity and character. Your extreme makeover involves a new walk, as you live in alignment with God's will. It involves a new talk, as your words reflect His truth and love. It brings a new heart, one filled with His compassion. It offers a new mind, as your thoughts are shaped by His wisdom. Your song is new, as you worship Him with joy and gratitude. You find new friends, those who share in your faith and purpose. And, most importantly, you receive a new soul, renewed and redeemed by God's grace.

2 Corinthians 5:17 (NIV) affirms this transformation, "Therefore, if anyone is in Christ, the new creation has come: The old has gone, the new is here!" It's a brand new life, not through your efforts, but through the work of God in you.

Your extreme makeover goes beyond the surface and penetrates the depths of your being. It's a transformation that can't be concealed; it radiates from your renewed heart and spirit. When God completes your turnaround, you become a living testament to His power and love, a living example of His grace. As you reflect on the phases of an industrial turnaround and the spiritual transformation God brings, may you embrace the profound and lasting change He has in store for you. You don't have to announce your makeover; it will radiate from within you as a testament to His transformative work in your life.

Decrees and Declarations

"I decree and declare that I am being made over again by the transforming power of God's love and grace, as stated in Ezekiel 36:26 (NIV)."

Scripture: Ezekiel 36:26 (NIV) - "I will give you a new heart and put a new spirit in you; I will remove from you your heart of stone and give you a heart of flesh."

"I decree and declare that, just as in a turnaround, God is purging, disassembling, pressure washing, repairing, and reassembling my life. I am becoming a new creation, as affirmed in 2 Corinthians 5:17 (NIV)."

Scripture: 2 Corinthians 5:17 (NIV) - "Therefore, if anyone is in Christ, the new creation has come: The old has gone, the new is here!"

"I decree and declare that my spiritual makeover is a profound transformation of my inner being, reflected in my walk, talk, heart, mind, song, friendships, and soul, in alignment with God's Word."

Scripture: Psalm 51:10 (NIV) - "Create in me a pure heart, O God, and renew a steadfast spirit within me."

"I decree and declare that my extreme makeover is not about outward appearances but a renewed heart and spirit, shining as a testament to God's transformative work."

Scripture: Romans 12:2 (NIV) - "Do not conform to the pattern of this world but be transformed by the renewing of your mind."

"I decree and declare that my life is a living example of God's power, love, and grace. My transformation radiates from within me, drawing others to His transformative work."

Scripture: Matthew 5:16 (NIV) - "In the same way, let your light shine before others, that they may see your good deeds and glorify your Father in heaven."

These decrees and declarations are founded on the promises of Scripture, affirming the profound makeover that God is working in our lives, from the inside out.

Prayer

Father,

We are reminded of the thorough and profound transformation that occurs when we undertake a turnaround in our lives. Your Word in Ezekiel 36:26 (NIV) tells us, "I will give you a new heart and put a new spirit in you; I will remove from you your heart of stone and give you a heart of flesh." We come before you, acknowledging the significance of this spiritual makeover in our lives.

Ezekiel 36:26 (NIV) assures us of the new heart and spirit you provide. We desire to be made over again, to shed the old and embrace the new that you offer.

Just as the phases of an industrial turnaround represent purging, disassembling, pressure washing, repairing, and reassembling, we recognize the profound work you are doing in our lives. Your Word in 2 Corinthians 5:17 (NIV) proclaims, "Therefore, if anyone is in Christ, the new creation has come: The old has gone, the new is here!" We declare this transformation in our lives. In this process, we decree and declare that we are becoming new creations. Just as the vessel is made ready to be powered up and operate within specification, we declare that we are being empowered by your Spirit. The old has gone; the new has come!

We affirm that our extreme makeover is not confined to outward appearances but is a profound transformation of our inner being. We declare, as Romans 12:2 (NIV) encourages, that our minds are being renewed and transformed by your grace. We decree and declare that our lives are a living testament to your power, love, and grace. Our transformation radiates from within us, drawing others to your transformative work. We claim the promise in Matthew 5:16 (NIV) to let our light shine before others so that they may see our good deeds and glorify you, our Father in heaven.

Heavenly Father, we surrender to your work in our lives, acknowledging the profound transformation you are bringing about. May our hearts, spirits, and entire beings be made over again by your love and grace.

In Jesus' name, we pray.

Amen.

- *12* -

Conflict Resolution

Turnaround is such a critical and complex aspect of the industrial organization that unexpected events and conflicts are bound to arise. In the high-performance world of team-based organizations, productive and creative collaboration is key. In successful organizations, teams face conflicts head-on. Conflict resolution is a structured process that involves identifying the problem, making a commitment to decisions, accepting one's role in the issue, and being willing to change behavior. This approach fosters an environment where conflicts are not hidden but addressed, leading to growth and success.

Similarly, in our relationship with God, we find the path to being free from conflict. It begins with recognizing the blessing of each new day and choosing to rejoice in it. Psalm 118:24 (NIV) encourages us, "This is the day the Lord has made; let us rejoice and be glad in it." We are called to find happiness in God, to relish life, and to enjoy the journey. Jesus himself promised an abundant life, as recorded in John 10:10 (NIV): "The thief comes only to steal and kill and destroy; I have come that they may have life, and have it to the full."

The approach to conflict resolution in a high-performance organization can serve as a model for how we can resolve conflicts and find peace and abundance in God. Let's explore how the principles align:

Identifying the Problem: In conflict resolution, defining the problem is the first step. Similarly, in our spiritual journey, recognizing our need for God and acknowledging areas of conflict in our lives is essential. Psalm 139:23-24 (NIV) guides us, "Search me, God, and know my heart; test me and know my anxious thoughts. See if there is any offensive way in me, and lead me in the way everlasting."

Committing to Decisions: In resolving conflicts, a commitment to decisions is crucial. In our relationship with God, committing to following His ways and decisions leads to peace. Proverbs 3:5-6 (NIV) offers wisdom: "Trust in the Lord with all your heart and lean not on your own understanding; in all your ways submit to him, and he will make your paths straight."

Accepting Responsibility: Conflict resolution often involves acknowledging one's part in the problem. Likewise, in our spiritual journey, recognizing our shortcomings and seeking forgiveness is a fundamental step. 1 John 1:9 (NIV) reassures us, "If we confess our sins, he is faithful and just and will forgive us our sins and purify us from all unrighteousness."

Willingness to Change: Conflict resolution requires a willingness to change behavior. In our walk with God, this transformation is at the core of our faith. Romans 12:2 (NIV) emphasizes, "Do not conform to the pattern of this world but be transformed by the renewing of your mind. Then you will be able to test and approve what God's will is—his good, pleasing and perfect will."

The path to conflict resolution in both the professional world and our spiritual journey involves an intentional and structured approach. It begins with identifying the issue, committing to Godly decisions, accepting our role, and being willing to change. This process is a transformative one, leading to growth, harmony, and success.

When we apply these principles to our relationship with God, the result is a life that overflows with abundance. As we rejoice in each new day, find happiness in God, and enjoy the journey, we experience the fullness of life that Jesus promised. It's not just about conflict resolution; it's about embracing the turnaround that God offers and seizing the moment to live life abundantly.

Philippians 4:6-7 (NIV) reassures us, "Do not be anxious about anything, but in every situation, by prayer and petition, with thanksgiving, present your requests to God. And the peace of God, which transcends all understanding, will guard your hearts and your minds in Christ Jesus." In God, we find the ultimate resolution to conflicts, the source of true peace, and the pathway to an abundant life.

The journey of faith is not without its challenges, but it is filled with opportunities for growth, transformation, and reconciliation. By adopting the principles of conflict resolution and rejoicing each day, we can experience the abundance of life that God intends for us.

Decrees and Declarations

"I decree and declare that, just as in conflict resolution, I will identify the problems and conflicts in my life and address them with the guidance of the Holy Spirit."

Scripture: Psalm 139:23-24 (NIV) - "Search me, God, and know my heart; test me and know my anxious thoughts. See if there is any offensive way in me, and lead me in the way everlasting."

"I decree and declare my commitment to following God's decisions and His ways, trusting that He will make my paths straight."

Scripture: Proverbs 3:5-6 (NIV) - "Trust in the Lord with all your heart and lean not on your own understanding; in all your ways submit to him, and he will make your paths straight."

I decree and declare that I will accept responsibility for my actions and seek God's forgiveness, knowing that He is faithful and just to forgive and purify me."

....

Scripture: 1 John 1:9 (NIV) - "If we confess our sins, he is faithful and just and will forgive us our sins and purify us from all unrighteousness."

"I decree and declare my willingness to change, to be transformed by the renewing of my mind according to God's will."

....

Scripture: Romans 12:2 (NIV) - "Do not conform to the pattern of this world but be transformed by the renewing of your mind. Then you will be able to test and approve what God's will is—his good, pleasing and perfect will."

"I decree and declare that in God, I find the ultimate resolution to conflicts, the source of true peace, and the pathway to an abundant life."

....

Scripture: Philippians 4:6-7 (NIV) - "Do not be anxious about anything, but in every situation, by prayer and petition, with thanksgiving, present your requests to God. And the peace of God, which transcends all understanding, will guard your hearts and your minds in Christ Jesus."

These decrees and declarations are grounded in the promises of Scripture, affirming our commitment to resolving conflicts and finding true peace and abundance in our relationship with God.

Prayer

Father,

We acknowledge the importance of addressing conflicts in our lives, just as high-performance teams do in their organizations. We are reminded that your Word provides guidance and principles for resolving conflicts and experiencing the abundant life you promise.

Psalm 139:23-24 (NIV) calls us to search our hearts, seeking your guidance: "Search me, God, and know my heart; test me and know my anxious thoughts. See if there is any offensive way in me, and lead me in the way everlasting." We come before you, seeking to identify the conflicts and issues in our lives and asking for your wisdom in resolving them.

Proverbs 3:5-6 (NIV) teaches us to trust in you with all our hearts: "Trust in the Lord with all your heart and lean not on your understanding; in all your ways submit to him, and he will make your paths straight." We commit to following your ways, trusting that You will guide us to the resolution of conflicts. We also declare that we will accept responsibility for our actions and seek your forgiveness, just as 1 John 1:9 (NIV) assures us: "If we confess our sins, he is faithful and just and will forgive us our sins and purify us from all unrighteousness."

Lord, we are willing to change and be transformed by the renewing of our minds, as Romans 12:2 (NIV) encourages us: "Do not conform to the pattern of this world but be transformed by the renewing of your mind. Then you will be able to test and approve what God's will is—his good, pleasing and perfect will." We open our hearts to your transformative work.

Finally, we acknowledge that true resolution and peace are found in You, as expressed in Philippians 4:6-7 (NIV): "Do not be anxious about anything, but in every situation, by prayer and petition, with thanksgiving, present your requests to God. And the peace of God, which transcends all understanding, will guard your hearts and your minds in Christ Jesus." We bring our conflicts before you, seeking your peace that surpasses all understanding.

Heavenly Father, we trust in your guidance, wisdom, and transformative power as we resolve conflicts in our lives. May your peace reign in our hearts, and may we experience the abundant life you promise.

In Jesus' name, we pray. Amen.

- *13* -

Communication

In the world of manufacturing, communication is a lifeline that ensures the smooth flow of operations. It is defined as a process by which information is exchanged between individuals through a common system of symbols, signs, or behavior. Effective communication is vital at all levels of an organization, especially in environments where the challenges of noise and distance require creative solutions, such as written procedures, instrument readings, hand signs, and radios. When communication is lacking or breaks down in any form, it can lead to friction and disrupt the entire system.

Similarly, God desires to be in constant communication with us, His beloved children. This divine communication involves prayer, meditation on His Word, belief, and action. It is a dynamic relationship where we not only read but also live out His Word. Just as communication is crucial in the manufacturing world, it is equally important in our relationship with God.

Prayer: Communication with God starts with prayer. 1 Thessalonians 5:17 (NIV) encourages us to "pray continually." Just as employees in manufacturing plants use hand signs or radios to bridge communication gaps, we are urged to maintain an ongoing conversation with our Heavenly Father.

Meditation on the Word: God's Word is a channel of communication between Him and us. Joshua 1:8 (NIV) instructs us, "Keep this Book of the Law always on your lips; meditate on it day and night so that you may be careful to do everything written in it." Just as industry relies on knowledge and adherence to effective written procedures, communication with God involves not just reading the Word but also internalizing its wisdom and guidance.

Belief and Action: True communication with God goes beyond words; it requires faith and action. As James 1:22 (NIV) reminds us, "Do not merely listen to the word, and so deceive yourselves. Do what it says." In a manufacturing setting, communication is not just about signals or radios; it's about acting on the information received. Similarly, in our relationship with God, belief and obedience are essential components of effective communication.

Praise and Worship: God not only desires communication through prayer and meditation but also through praise and worship. Psalm 22:3 (NIV) states, "But you are holy, enthroned in the praises of Israel." Just as personnel in a manufacturing plant rely on communication and feedback to maintain morale, order and efficiency, we honor God by acknowledging His greatness and expressing our love and reverence through worship.

Family Communication: In the manufacturing industry, there is a concern about the high divorce rate among shift workers, highlighting the importance of family communication. This concern mirrors God's desire for families to stay together. Effective family communication strengthens relationships and fosters an environment of love and support.

Our relationship with God is a model for communication that extends beyond human understanding. In 1 Thessalonians 5:18 (NIV), we are encouraged to "give thanks in all circumstances; for this is God's will for you in Christ Jesus." This all-encompassing communication with God reflects His desire to be present in our lives, guiding, comforting, and transforming us.

Just as communication breakdowns disrupt manufacturing processes, a lack of communication with God can lead to spiritual disconnection. It is through effective communication that we bridge the gaps between our human limitations and God's boundless wisdom and love.

Communication is the cornerstone of a well-functioning organization. Our communication with God is the cornerstone of a purposeful and fulfilled life. The principles of communication are not confined to human interactions but extend to our divine relationship with our Creator, making it the most vital form of communication we will ever engage in.

Decrees and Declarations

"I decree and declare that I will maintain constant communication with God through unceasing prayer, just as 1 Thessalonians 5:17 (NIV) encourages: 'pray continually.'"

"I decree and declare that I will meditate on God's Word day and night, internalizing His wisdom and actively living out His guidance, in obedience to Joshua 1:8 (NIV): 'Keep this Book of the Law always on your lips; meditate on it day and night so that you may be careful to do everything written in it.'"

"I decree and declare that I will not only be a hearer but also a doer of God's Word, as James 1:22 (NIV) admonishes: 'Do not merely listen to the word, and so deceive yourselves. Do what it says.'"

"I decree and declare that I will engage in continuous praise and worship, acknowledging God's holiness and dwelling in His presence, as stated in Psalm 22:3 (NIV): 'But you are holy, enthroned in the praises of Israel.'"

"I decree and declare that my family will be a place of open and loving communication, mirroring God's desire for families to stay together and thrive."

....

These decrees and declarations are firmly rooted in Scripture, affirming our commitment to maintaining effective communication with God and within our families, as well as living out His Word with unwavering faith and obedience.

Prayer

Father,

We recognize the profound importance of communication in our lives, both with one another and with you. Your Word reminds us that communication is a lifeline that binds us together in understanding and harmony. 1 Thessalonians 5:17 (NIV) instructs us to "pray continually." We embrace this decree by committing to maintain an unceasing conversation with you, our loving Father. Just as effective communication is vital in the functioning of an organization, may our prayers be a source of connection and guidance.

Joshua 1:8 (NIV) calls us to meditate on your Word day and night, living out its wisdom in our daily lives. We pray for the strength and dedication to internalize your guidance, being both hearers and doers of your Word. James 1:22 (NIV) reminds us not to deceive ourselves by merely listening but to do what your Word says. We declare our commitment to obediently follow your Word, allowing it to transform our hearts and actions.

Psalm 22:3 (NIV) proclaims that you are holy and enthroned in the praises of your people. We pledge to engage in continuous praise and worship, acknowledging your holiness, and dwelling in your presence through music and adoration.

Lord, we also recognize the significance of family communication.

We pray that our families become a sanctuary of open and loving communication, reflecting your desire for families to remain united and strong. In our communication, we seek to bridge the gap between our human limitations and your boundless wisdom and love. Just as an organization relies on effective communication to function, we depend on the channel of communication with you, our Creator, to lead purposeful and fulfilled lives.

May our communication with you be a source of strength, wisdom, and intimacy. In times of joy and challenges, we strive to follow your will and maintain an unbroken connection with you. We are grateful for the lessons and wisdom found in your Word, which guide our communication with You and with one another.

In Jesus' name, we pray.

Amen.

14

Stress Relief

In the demanding world we live in, stress has become a prevalent issue, often building up like pressure in a container. When stress reaches a dangerous level, it can take a toll on our physical, emotional, and spiritual well-being. It is not uncommon to engage flares and pressure relief valves as a safety net during turnarounds. Just as a relief valve opens automatically to release pressure in a container, we need effective ways to alleviate the stress that threatens to overwhelm us.

The Overwhelming Impact of Stress

Statistics reveal the widespread impact of stress on our lives. In the United States, 30 million men describe themselves as "stressed out." The average desk worker has a staggering 36 hours of work on their desk, spending three hours each week simply sorting through the piles. Middle managers are interrupted 73 times a day, leading to increased stress levels and decreased productivity. We spend an average of eight months of our lives opening junk mail, two years trying to call unavailable people, and one year searching for misplaced objects, even if they are only a short distance away.

The weight of these statistics reflects the very real and detrimental effects of stress on our lives. When we allow stress to build up without a relief valve, it can lead to physical health issues, emotional strain, and a strain on our relationships. But there is a solution to this overwhelming stress, and it is found in our faith in God.

Prayer as a Relief Valve

In times of stress, we can turn to prayer as our relief valve. In Philippians 4:6-7 (NIV), we are encouraged: "Do not be anxious about anything, but in every situation, by prayer and petition, with thanksgiving, present your requests to God. And the peace of God, which transcends all understanding, will guard your hearts and your minds in Christ Jesus."

Prayer is a powerful means of releasing the pressure of stress. It allows us to bring our concerns, fears, and anxieties before God, who is the ultimate source of relief. By surrendering our burdens to Him, we find a peace that goes beyond human comprehension. This divine peace serves as our relief valve, guarding our hearts and minds from the overwhelming effects of stress.

Praise and Worship as Stress Relief

Praise and worship are equally powerful forms of stress relief. In Psalm 100:2 (NIV), we are instructed: "Worship the Lord with gladness; come before him with joyful songs." The act of praising and worshiping God provides an avenue for us to express gratitude and joy, even during stressful circumstances.

Stress often makes us want to pop open like a relief valve, but praise and worship direct our focus toward God. They remind us of His goodness, faithfulness, and sovereignty. By magnifying His presence in our lives, we find relief from the weight of stress, as we align our hearts with His peace and joy.

Finding Relief in God

Ultimately, the relief we seek from stress is found in God. As the psalmist proclaims in Psalm 34:4 (NIV), "I sought the Lord, and he answered me; he delivered me from all my fears." When we seek God in prayer, praise, and worship, we discover that He is our ultimate source of relief. He delivers us from fear, anxiety, and the overwhelming pressure of stress.

The acronym for relief, G-O-D (God Our Deliverer), beautifully encapsulates this concept. God is our relief valve in times of stress. Through prayer, praise, and worship, we open the valve and release the pressure, allowing God's peace to fill our hearts and minds. Just as a relief valve prevents a container from bursting under pressure, God safeguards our well-being, providing us with the strength to overcome stress and find peace in Him.

In a world that often feels inundated by stress, we can turn to God as our relief valve. He offers us the peace that surpasses all understanding, guarding our hearts and minds. Prayer, praise, and worship serve as powerful means to release the pressure of stress and find solace in His presence. Just as a relief valve prevents a container from bursting under pressure, God safeguards our well-being and offers relief during life's challenges. With God as our ultimate source of relief, we can find peace and serenity even in the most stressful of times.

Decrees and Declarations

"I decree and declare that I will not be anxious about anything, as stated in Philippians 4:6 (NIV), but in every situation, I will turn to prayer and present my requests to God with thanksgiving, finding peace that transcends all understanding to guard my heart and mind in Christ Jesus."

"I decree and declare that stress has no power over me, for I trust in the promise of Psalm 34:4 (NIV): 'I sought the Lord, and he answered me; he delivered me from all my fears.' I seek the Lord in times of stress, finding deliverance and freedom from fear."

....

"I decree and declare that, just as a relief valve prevents a container from bursting under pressure, I will open the valve of praise and worship in my life. I will worship the Lord with gladness and come before Him with joyful songs, as instructed in Psalm 100:2 (NIV)."

....

"I decree and declare that stress will not overwhelm me, for I know that stress often makes us want to 'pop open' like a relief valve. However, I choose to rely on God as my ultimate relief valve, finding refuge and strength in His presence."

....

"I decree and declare that, by following the wisdom of Ecclesiastes 4:6-7 (NIV), I will not allow stress to burden my life. Instead, I will turn to God in prayer, bringing my concerns and anxieties before Him, and in return, His peace, which transcends understanding, will guard my heart and mind."

....

These decrees and declarations center around the principles of seeking God's peace and relief in times of stress, as prescribed in various Scriptures. They reinforce the idea that stress can be overcome through faith, prayer, praise, and worship, drawing strength from God as the ultimate relief valve.

Prayer

Father,

As we come before your presence, we acknowledge the stress that often tries to overwhelm us in the challenges of life. Your Word reminds us of the relief and peace we can find in you, just as a relief valve releases pressure. We turn to you in prayer, knowing that you are the ultimate source of comfort and tranquility.

We heed the counsel of Philippians 4:6 (NIV), which instructs us not to be anxious but to bring our concerns to you in prayer and with thanksgiving. We trust that, as we present our requests to you, the peace that transcends all understanding will guard our hearts and minds in Christ Jesus.

We claim the promise of Psalm 34:4 (NIV), that when we seek you, you answer us and deliver us from all our fears. In times of stress, we seek your presence, knowing that you are our refuge and our strength.

We lift our voices in praise and worship, as described in Psalm 100:2 (NIV), coming before you with joyful songs. We recognize that, just as a relief valve releases pressure, our praise and worship release the burdens of stress, filling our hearts with gratitude and joy.

We trust in your protection and strength, understanding that you are our ultimate relief valve. You prevent us from bursting under the pressure of life's challenges. As a relief valve safeguards a container, you safeguard our well-being.

Heavenly Father, we thank you for being our relief valve in times of stress. We find solace in the promise of your Word, and we rely on the power of prayer, praise, and worship to release the pressure of stress in our lives. Just as a relief valve prevents a container from bursting, you safeguard our hearts and minds, offering peace that surpasses all understanding.

May our faith in you be our constant source of relief, guarding us against the overwhelming effects of stress. In the name of Jesus, we pray.

Amen.

15

Obedience

Adherence to instructions and procedures plays a critical role in manufacturing, helping to prevent catastrophe. In the journey of faith and spiritual transformation, obedience to God stands as a fundamental pillar. It is through obedience that we align our lives with the divine will. When we listen to God and follow His commands, we prevent spiritual destruction and find ourselves on the path of blessing and renewal.

Obedience as an Act of Listening

Obedience to God begins with attentive listening. In Deuteronomy 30:8 (NIV), we are reminded: "You will again obey the Lord and follow all his commands I am giving you today." Obedience is a result of listening to God's commands and aligning our actions with His will.

Just as industrial processes require attention to signs and sounds in vessels to prevent major destruction, we, too, need to listen to God's guidance and avoid spiritual destruction. It is through this obedient listening that we maintain a strong connection with our Creator.

The Relationship Between Listening and Obedience

In industry, the practice of listening helps prevent catastrophic failures. Similarly, in our spiritual lives, listening to God leads to obedience and the avoidance of destructive paths. The relationship between listening and obedience is reflected in John 10:27 (NIV): "My sheep listen to my voice; I know them, and they follow me."

As God's sheep, we are called to listen to His voice and obey His commands. It is through this obedient listening that we follow the Good Shepherd, avoiding the pitfalls of disobedience and spiritual turmoil.

The Consequences of Disobedience

Consider the lessons from Israel's history in 1 Samuel 15. Saul failed to completely destroy the Amalekites as commanded by God. As a result, God rejected Saul as king. Israel's recurring failure to obey God's commands brought about severe consequences. God consistently blessed their obedience, but their continuous disobedience led to misery and eventual downfall. Just as disobedience brought hardships to God's covenant people, it can likewise disrupt our relationship with God and lead to spiritual distress.

Commitment to Obedience

What would it take for you to disobey God? The answer should be a resounding commitment to unwavering obedience. Your commitment to God should be non-negotiable. As 1 Samuel 15:22 (NIV) states, "Does the Lord delight in burnt offerings and sacrifices as much as in obeying the Lord? To obey is better than sacrifice." God values obedience above religious rituals or empty sacrifices. Our commitment to obeying His commands should be steadfast and unwavering.

The Path of Blessing

Obedience leads us on the path of blessing and renewal. In Deuteronomy 28:2 (NIV), we find the promise: "All these blessings will come on you and accompany you if you obey the Lord your God." Obedience to God's commands results in His favor and blessings in our lives.

Just as listening to sounds in vessels helps prevent major destruction in manufacturing, listening to God and obeying His commands prevent spiritual destruction. Obedience aligns us with God's will, safeguarding our spiritual journey and ensuring that we experience the fullness of His blessings.

Obedience to God is not merely a religious obligation; it is a vital component of a vibrant and thriving relationship with our Creator. Just as listening plays a crucial role in manufacturing, obedient listening to God's voice prevents spiritual destruction and leads to a life marked by His blessings and renewal.

In considering the biblical lessons from Israel's history, we recognize that habitual disobedience brings misery and eventual downfall. Therefore, we are called to maintain a steadfast commitment to obeying God, making it non-negotiable in our lives. Our obedience paves the way for blessings and a deeper connection with the divine.

As we continue our journey of spiritual transformation, let us remember that obedience is a cornerstone of our faith, just as listening is a vital tool in industry. Through obedient listening, we prevent spiritual destruction and remain on the path to God's favor and renewal.

Watching is vital in the chemical industry, as well as spiritual transformation. A good operator does not wait for failure, they observe trends. Spiritually watching means paying attention to thoughts, motives, and attitudes. It means being alert to God's movement and warnings. Watching is preventive, not reactive. In industry, early detection prevents shutdowns. In faith, early awareness prevents spiritual erosion.

Unchecked pressure destroys vessels and unchecked pride, bitterness, or complacency destroys character. A plant operator watches because lives depend on it. A Christian watches because souls depend on it.

Decrees and Declarations

"I decree and declare that I will listen to God's voice attentively, as stated in Deuteronomy 30:8 (NIV). I will follow His commands and walk in obedience, aligning my life with His divine will, and I will be blessed in all I do."

"I decree and declare that I will listen to God's guidance to prevent spiritual destruction. As His sheep, I will listen to His voice, know Him, and follow Him, as declared in John 10:27 (NIV)."

"I decree and declare that obedience to God is my unwavering commitment, as emphasized in 1 Samuel 15:22 (NIV). I understand that obeying the Lord is better than any sacrifice, and I will prioritize obedience above all else in my relationship with Him."

"I decree and declare that, through my obedience to God's commands, I will experience the path of blessing and renewal, as promised in Deuteronomy 28:2 (NIV). I am committed to living a life marked by His favor and the fullness of His blessings."

"I decree and declare that obedience to God is the cornerstone of my faith. Obedient listening to God's voice is vital to my spiritual journey. I will remain obedient to prevent spiritual destruction and stay on the path of God's favor and renewal."

"I decree and declare that I will **watch and remain spiritually alert**, discerning the times and seasons of my life, as instructed in 1 Peter

5:8 (NIV). I will be sober-minded and vigilant, guarding my heart, thoughts, and actions. I will not ignore subtle warnings or spiritual shifts, but I will remain attentive to God's guidance, allowing the Holy Spirit to reveal what needs correction, adjustment, or growth in my life."

....

These decrees and declarations focus on the importance of obedience to God, drawing parallels with listening and watching in manufacturing to emphasize the significance of obedient listening and watching in our spiritual lives. They highlight the commitment to prioritize obedience, understanding that it leads to blessings and a deeper connection with God.

Prayer

Heavenly Father,

As we come before your presence, we acknowledge the importance of obedience in our journey of faith. Your Word teaches us the significance of listening to your voice and following your commands. We recognize that obedient listening to you is vital to prevent spiritual destruction and lead us on the path of blessing.

Obedience as Attentive Listening

We heed the wisdom of Deuteronomy 30:8 (NIV), "You will again obey the Lord and follow all his commands I am giving you today." Obedience begins with listening to your voice and aligning our lives with your divine will.

Listening and Following Your Guidance

We acknowledge the relationship between listening and obedience, In John 10:27 (NIV), Jesus states, "My sheep listen to my voice; I know them, and they follow me." We, too, desire to be your sheep, listening to your voice, knowing you, and faithfully following your guidance.

Unwavering Commitment to Obedience

We decree that our commitment to obedience is unwavering, as proclaimed in 1 Samuel 15:22 (NIV).

We understand that obedience to You is better than any sacrifice, and we prioritize this commitment above all else in our walk with You. Just as attentive listening and watching are crucial in manufacturing for ensuring safety and quality, we recognize that our spiritual journey requires us to be alert and responsive to Your guidance. By remaining focused on Your voice and faithfully following Your instructions, we position ourselves to receive Your blessings and deepen our relationship with You. Help us, Lord, to continually choose obedience, trusting that it leads us into greater purpose and fulfillment in You.

The Path of Blessing

We declare that through our obedience to your commands, we will experience the path of blessing and renewal, as promised in Deuteronomy 28:2 (NIV). We are committed to living lives marked by your favor and the fullness of your blessings.

Heavenly Father, we understand that obedience is a cornerstone of our faith. Through obedient listening to your voice, we prevent spiritual destruction and remain on the path of your favor and renewal. May our commitment to obedience be unwavering, and may we always Prioritize obedient listening to you, knowing that it leads to blessings and a deeper connection with you. As we continue our journey of faith, help us to obey your commands faithfully, just as we listen attentively to your voice.

Lord, help us to watch with a discerning heart and walk in obedient alignment with your will, attentive to Your voice and faithful in every step You direct.

In the name of Jesus, we pray. Amen.

- 16 -

Maintenance

In the journey of faith and spiritual transformation, the process of maintenance is vital to ensure that the gains made through the turnaround process are sustained. Just as in manufacturing where preventive maintenance is essential to prevent equipment breakdown, preventive maintenance in our spiritual lives involves knowing and believing in the promises of God. These promises are our guarantee of continued growth and prosperity.

The Role of Faith in Maintenance

Faith in God is the key to maintaining the progress achieved in the turnaround process. Just as maintenance ensures the continuous smooth operation of equipment in manufacturing, faith in God ensures the ongoing vitality of our spiritual lives. The Bible tells us in Hebrews 11:1 (NIV) that "faith is confidence in what we hope for and assurance about what we do not see." It is through faith that we sustain our spiritual growth and the blessings that come with it.

Faith comes by knowing and believing in the promises of God. These promises serve as guarantees or agreements made by God to His people. One such promise is found in Jeremiah 29:11 (NIV): "For I know the plans I have for you," declares the Lord, "plans to prosper you and not to harm you, plans to give you hope and a future."

Believing in and holding onto these promises acts as preventive maintenance in our faith journey. When we are assured of God's plans to prosper us and provide us with hope and a future, we can navigate life's challenges with confidence.

Maintaining Spiritual Growth

Just as machinery needs constant upkeep to function optimally, our spiritual lives require continuous maintenance. In industry, routine maintenance is instituted to prevent equipment failure and costly repairs. Similarly, in our spiritual lives, we can institute preventive maintenance with practices such as prayer, reading and meditating on God's Word, and maintaining a close relationship with Him. Proverbs 3:5-6 (NIV) reminds us: "Trust in the Lord with all your heart and lean not on your own understanding; in all your ways submit to him, and he will make your paths straight."

By trusting in the Lord and submitting to His guidance, we ensure that our spiritual path remains on the right track. The maintenance of our faith is an ongoing process, and it relies on our commitment to staying connected to our Creator.

The Impact of Promises in Preventive Maintenance

Promises from God serve as anchors in our spiritual lives. Just as manufacturing equipment can function optimally when property maintained, our faith thrives when anchored in God's promises. One such promise is Philippians 4:19 (NIV): "And my God will meet all your needs according to the riches of his glory in Christ Jesus." Believing in this promise provides assurance that God will meet our needs, and this knowledge is integral to our spiritual maintenance.

The Cycle of Spiritual Maintenance

In industry, maintenance is an ongoing cycle, with regular inspections, repairs, and adjustments. Likewise, our spiritual maintenance is continuous. Regular communion with God, seeking His guidance, and holding onto His promises are integral parts of this cycle.

In our faith journey, maintenance is essential for preserving the gains made in the turnaround process. Faith in God plays a central role in this maintenance, as it provides the assurance and confidence necessary for spiritual growth. Just as preventive maintenance in manufacturing prevents equipment failure, knowing and believing in God's promises serves as preventive maintenance for our faith.

We are called to maintain our spiritual lives through practices like prayer, reading scripture, and staying connected with God. Promises from God are our guarantees of continued growth and prosperity, and they act as anchors in our faith journey. As we navigate the cycle of spiritual maintenance, may our faith remain vibrant and our connection with God grow stronger with each passing day.

Decrees and Declarations

"I decree and declare that faith in God is my cornerstone for maintaining the gains achieved in the turnaround process, as proclaimed in Hebrews 11:1 (NIV). I have confidence in what I hope for and assurance in what I do not see, securing the continuity of my spiritual growth."

"I decree and declare that, just as preventive maintenance is instituted in industry to prevent equipment failure, I will institute preventive maintenance in my spiritual life by holding onto the promises of God. These promises are my guarantees for ongoing growth and prosperity, as revealed in Jeremiah 29:11 (NIV)."

"I decree and declare that my faith journey involves continuous maintenance, as our spiritual lives require regular upkeep, just like machinery. I will trust in the Lord with all my heart, not leaning on my understanding, and in all my ways, I will submit to Him, as guided by Proverbs 3:5-6 (NIV)."

....

"I decree and declare that promises from God serve as anchors in my spiritual life, just as maintenance ensures optimal equipment function. Believing in God's promises, such as Philippians 4:19 (NIV), assures me that He will meet all my needs according to His riches in Christ Jesus."

....

"I decree and declare that spiritual maintenance is an ongoing cycle in my faith journey, with regular communion with God, seeking His guidance, and holding onto His promises. Just as in manufacturing, I will maintain my faith to preserve the gains made in the turnaround process."

....

These decrees and declarations emphasize the role of faith, preventive maintenance through God's promises, and the continuous cycle of spiritual maintenance. They serve as affirmations to ensure the ongoing vitality of one's spiritual life, just as maintenance is essential to keep machinery functioning optimally.

Prayer

Heavenly Father,

As we gather before your presence, we acknowledge the importance of maintenance in our spiritual journey. We are reminded that, just as in industry, maintenance is essential to ensure the continued operation and growth of our faith. We come to you, seeking guidance and strength for this vital aspect of our walk with you.

The Role of Faith in Maintenance

We understand, Lord, that faith in you is the cornerstone of maintaining the gains achieved in our turnaround process. We draw from Hebrews 11:1 (NIV), which teaches us that faith is confidence in what we hope for and assurance about what we do not see. We place our confidence in you, knowing that through faith, we can secure the continuity of our spiritual growth.

Preventive Maintenance through Your Promises

We acknowledge that preventive maintenance in our spiritual lives requires that we be vigilant, alert and watchful. It requires knowing and believing in your promises. Your promises are our guarantees of ongoing growth and prosperity, as affirmed in Jeremiah 29:11 (NIV). We are grateful for the assurance that your plans for us are to prosper and provide hope and a future.

The Maintenance of Our Faith

Just as manufacturing equipment requires ongoing maintenance, our spiritual lives also demand continuous upkeep. We commit to maintaining our faith through practices such as prayer, reading your Word, and staying closely connected to you. We lean on the wisdom of Proverbs 3:5-6 (NIV), trusting in you with all our hearts and submitting to your guidance.

Anchored in Your Promises

We declare that your promises serve as anchors in our spiritual lives, just as maintenance ensures optimal equipment function. Your promise in Philippians 4:19 (NIV), that you will meet all our needs according to the riches of your glory in Christ Jesus, provides us with the assurance that you are our Provider.

The Cycle of Spiritual Maintenance

We recognize that the cycle of spiritual maintenance is continuous, involving regular communion with you, seeking your guidance, and holding onto your promises. We commit to maintaining our spiritual lives, preserving the gains made in the turnaround process.

Heavenly Father, as we embark on the journey of spiritual maintenance, we seek your strength and wisdom. We place our trust in your faithfulness and rely on your promises. May our faith remain vibrant and our connection with You grow stronger with each passing day.

In the name of Jesus, we pray.

Amen.

Afterword

Finding a church to call your spiritual home is a journey that requires prayer, discernment, and alignment with your beliefs and values. This crucial step in your faith journey is not just a matter of convenience but a reflection of your commitment to God and your desire to stay focused on Him. Let us explore the process of finding a church through the lens of scripture and consider the practical steps and questions that can guide you on this sacred quest.

What Are My Beliefs?

The foundation of finding a church begins with your core beliefs and values. 1 Corinthians 1:10 (NIV) reminds us, "I appeal to you, brothers and sisters, in the name of our Lord Jesus Christ, that all of you agree with one another in what you say and that there be no divisions among you, but that you be perfectly united in mind and thought." Seek a church whose doctrine aligns with your faith and values.

What Type of Service Structure Do I Prefer?

Service structures can vary widely, from traditional to contemporary.

your preference may be influenced by your personality and spiritual needs. Psalm 33:3 (NIV) speaks of a new song and instruments of ten strings, showing the diversity of worship styles.

What Type of Worship Best Suits Me?

Worship style can greatly impact your connection with God. John 4:24 (NIV) highlights the importance of worshiping in spirit and truth. Choose a church where you can authentically connect with God in your worship.

What Types of Ministries and Programs Are Offered?

Consider the ministries and programs offered by the church. 1 Corinthians 12:4-7 (NIV) explains that there are different kinds of gifts but the same Spirit. Look for a church where you can utilize your gifts to serve and grow.

What Type of Youth Programs Are Offered?

If you have children or grandchildren, explore the youth programs available. Proverbs 22:6 (NIV) encourages the training of children in the way they should go. A church with strong youth programs can be a valuable resource.

Do I Prefer a Small or a Large Church?

Matthew 18:20 (NIV) assures us that where two or three gather in Christ's name, He is with them. The size of the church is less important than the sincerity of the community. Choose the size that makes you feel connected and comfortable.

What Type of Attire Would I Be Most Comfortable Wearing to Church?

1 Samuel 16:7 (NIV) reminds us that God looks at the heart, not the outward appearance. Choose a church where you can come as you are and feel comfortable in your attire.

Talk to the Pastor:

Hebrews 13:17 (NIV) encourages us to obey our leaders and submit to their authority. Talking to the pastor can provide insights into the church's vision, leadership, and values.

Visit Church Websites:

In today's digital age, many churches have websites that offer information about their beliefs, services, and activities. Proverbs 18:15 (NIV) emphasizes the importance of acquiring knowledge.

Make a Checklist:

Create a checklist of your preferences, beliefs, and priorities when choosing a church. Proverbs 16:3 (NIV) encourages committing your plans to the Lord.

Prayer, Discernment, and Alignment with Scripture:

Throughout this journey, seek guidance from God, for Proverbs 3:5-6 (NIV) assures us, "Trust in the Lord with all your heart and lean not on your understanding; in all your ways submit to him, and he will make your paths straight." As you embark on this quest to find a church, know that it is a place where you can gather, worship, learn, serve, and unite with a community of fellow believers.

Hebrews 10:25 (NIV) urges us not to forsake gathering together, as some are in the habit of doing, but to encourage one another. May your search for a church be guided by the Word of God and lead you to a community where you can continue to grow in your faith and serve the Lord.

In the end, remember that God's guidance, prayer, and the alignment of your beliefs with the church's doctrine are paramount. Trust in His wisdom, and He will lead you to the place where you can best serve and worship Him, staying focused on your faith journey.

Amen.

About the Author

Cheryl January is a marketplace minister with a calling to reach the lost beyond the four walls of the church, meeting people in workplaces, grocery stores, school events, and everyday spaces where faith intersects with real life. She is an Aspiring Mssionary and serves on the Evangelism Team at Starlight Church of God in Christ. Cheryl is currently pursuing a Doctor of Theology degree from Ruach School of Theology.

She holds an Associate Degree in Occupational Safety and Health, an Associate Degree in Process Technology, a Bachelor of Social Work, an MBA in Management, and a Master's Degree in Information Systems. Her professional background spans both industry and education. Cheryl worked at Goodyear Tire and Rubber as a Process Operator and in Organizational Development, gaining direct experience in high-risk, high-accountability environments.

In higher education, she served as the Director of Industrial Systems at Lamar State College Orange, where she led workforce and technical programs. After retiring from that leadership role, she returned to Lamar State College Orange as a full-time Instructor, teaching Process Technology courses and mentoring students entering the industrial workforce.

Cheryl January is a 2023 Woman of Valour honoree from Houston, Texas. She is also the founder of Community Keepers, a service-oriented group dedicated to meeting practical needs within her local community. Through faith, service, education, and industry experience, Cheryl bridges the sacred and the secular, demonstrating that ministry happens wherever people live, work, and struggle.

www.ingramcontent.com/pod-product-compliance
Lightning Source LLC
Chambersburg PA
CBHW020425130626
46549CB00006B/2749